Garage Sale Buddha

*A Maverick Minister's
Marginally Cultured
Pearls of Wisdom*

THOMAS DICKELMAN

Garage Sale Buddha
A Maverick Minister's Marginally
Cultured Pearls of Wisdom

Published by Across the Lake Publishing Company, LLC
Copyright © 2022 by Thomas S. Dickelman
www.garagesalebuddha.com

Cover Inspired by Bill Bartolotta
Cover Photo by Barbara Morley
Interior Layout by Kraig W. Moreland
Cover Design by Phillip Ross
Back Cover Portrait by Kerri Sherman

ISBN: 978-1-7322251-9-0

Across the Lake Publishing Co., LLC
Lake Bluff, IL

Dedication

This book is dedicated to family—to four distinct families. First, my family of origin, in particular my mom and dad, who gave me a wonderful childhood and loving support throughout my life.

Second, the family that I share with my wife, Jean, which includes Tommy, Kate, and Annie (and some seriously spoiled animals). They've loved and encouraged me over the years amidst the ongoing challenges of starting and leading a church.

Third, the Community Church family that for over two decades has nurtured and loved me, and—in some cases—put up with me. I have been privileged to serve such a wonderfully open-minded and spirited community.

Finally, this book is dedicated to the families over the years that have adopted me. Families who've loved me as one of their own, and helped me find my way over, around, or through life's hurdles.

Table of Contents

Introduction

Introduction

Doing research in 2020 for my third unfinished book while visiting my sister Sue and her husband Brian in Florida

"You should write a book!" is a comment I've received over the years after people have heard bits and pieces of my story. My typical response?

"I have! I've just never felt anything I've written has been worth reading, let alone publishing."

My first attempt at writing a book was titled *Even if You Win the Rat Race...You're Still a Rat.* My goal was to capture the vision I had for life and ministry in our super fast-paced, too-many-balls-up-in-the-air culture. I was going to be *different*, and live a life balancing all that mattered to me: family, faith, friends, fun, work, etc. The problem was that over time, amidst my quest to support our family and build a church that worked, it became painfully clear that I was an abysmal failure at being different—and had become a big-time rat myself. Rather than getting others to march in the balanced life parade I envisioned, I was marching to the lopsided drumbeat of work, work, work that's normative for so many in our communities. Let's just say if I had finished the book, it would have been in the fiction section of the local library.

My second attempt at becoming an author was titled *Doin' the God Thing.* I tried to put on paper what is foundational to the Community Church—helping people move toward authentic faith. I loved the process of writing the book, particularly the research which forced me to think through what, after nearly four decades of ministry, I truly felt about the spiritual life.

The problem came when I finished the draft and set my work aside for a few months. Upon reviewing what I had written, it appeared that I had really written two mini-books. One, an introduction to faith for people who'd lived outside the church, and two, what could only be called "Tom's Wacky Ministry Stories." I decided to put the project on hold—though if I can collect enough wacky ministry stories (which these days does not seem to be a problem) between now and someday I may resurrect *Doin' the God Thing.*

My final, untitled book began in earnest in 2020. While I have played golf all my life, in recent years I've rediscovered the love I had for the game as a young man. The challenge is that golf does not appear to love me as much as I love golf. In short, I suck.

The solution to transform my golf game once and for all? It was to spend one year (a) reading everything I could about golf, including classics such as Harvey Penick's *Little Red Book* as well as Bob Rotella's *Golf is Not a Game of Perfect,* and Deepak Chopra's *Golf for Enlightenment,* (b) watching the mountainous collection of instructional videos available, and

(c) chart what I learned every time I practiced or played. In short, I wanted to become as knowledgeable and skilled as possible—without taking lessons. And I'd write a book about my journey, which I of course assumed would be successful.

Unfortunately, my golf writing project petered out in the autumn of 2020 as the pandemic, big changes at the Community Church, and, most of all, my sister Sue's battle with cancer became top priorities. I plan to return to this project at some stage, because it seems like fun and based on my most recent round…I still suck at golf.

As for *this book*—take four? I've decided to give writing one more try as I approach the 18th hole of my ministry because I enjoy it, and as the saying goes, "So I know what I think." And, while I hope you appreciate the vignettes on the following pages, the truth is I've written this book because of the value I've found in reflecting on my life and work. It's brought great joy and a deep sense of gratitude, but it has also put me face to face with the countless times I've tripped and fallen short of being the person God calls me to be—or who I want to be.

The bottom line? This small book provides you with a chance to eavesdrop on the stories, faith, and thinking that have joined to form a unique life. Included are very personal narratives of powerful and pivotal decisions and experiences, as well as lighter moments of unabashed joy—all viewed through my unconventional lens.

In *Garage Sale Buddha*, you'll get what my friend David Spadafora, the former President of Lake Forest College said of me one Sunday while he was preaching to our congregation. "There's regular Tom and there's wacky Tom," he offered, "and you never know which one you are going to get."

You get both. And, amidst the "smorgasbord of tidbits" I've compiled, my hope is that you will find a meal.

- TD 2022

Spirit

The sunrise before our final Worship on the Beach Service of 2021

Garage Sale Buddha

In our home there is a small nook built into the wall, about 12 inches deep, 12 inches wide, and 20 inches high. Sitting peacefully inside, as if designed for it, is an untypically thin, smiling Buddha adorned with faux emeralds and diamonds. Appearing comfortably cross-legged beneath the glow of a hidden light, Buddha radiates a welcoming vibe to all who walk past.

We bought Buddha for $10 at a garage sale.

While I'm typically not a "garage sailor," I will be forever grateful we stopped by a neighborhood sale one Saturday when my wife Jean and I found Buddha. Why? Because it's one of the best things that's happened to my prayer life in a long time.

You see, adjacent Buddha—sitting in the base of a window about two feet away—is a Tibetan Prayer Wheel I purchased in Kathmandu in 2015. One day, with no real forethought, I began a ritual that has stuck. When I walk past, I touch Buddha's outstretched hand and spin the Tibetan Prayer Wheel while offering a one-line prayer to God of what is foremost in my mind.

"Lord, may your healing presence be with Sue battling cancer."

"Bless Kate and Annie with a safe trip this summer."

"Help me understand how to help Ted right now."

It's become such a valued ritual that I literally cannot walk past without touching Buddha's hand, spinning the wheel, and saying a prayer.

It goes without saying that an ordained Presbyterian minister with universalist leanings serving an independent church who prays multiple times each day by touching

Buddha and spinning a Tibetan Prayer Wheel from Kathmandu may be a little wacky.

Welcome to my world. It's a world where our church has no building, members, or committees. Where each summer for four months we worship on the beach. Where there's no choir but we're known for spectacular music. Where our flavor of Christianity intentionally respects and honors other traditions, exemplified by our omnipresent prayer flags. Where business principles have driven much of the unlikely success we've experienced. And where amidst our wackiness, we continue to blossom.

I love the Buddha and Prayer Wheel ritual because it evolved organically. With every prayer, I stay in touch with what matters most in my life. It helps me be who God calls me to be. And, as with all prayer, it doesn't necessarily change the world—but it does change me.

Be Who You Are

The late Rev. Forrest Church developed a three-line mantra as part of his alcohol recovery program. The mantra effectively guided him the last ten years of his life, and goes like this:

- Want what you have.
- Do what you can.
- Be who you are.

The final line—be who you are—at first sounds a little silly. Be who you are. *Duh*. What is that supposed to mean? Yet upon reflection, "be who you are" sums up much of what our lives are about—figuring out who we are, who we yearn to be, and, for some of us, who we feel God calls us to be.

For me, figuring out who I am has been a ridiculously long and sometimes absurd struggle. I've waged countless unnecessary battles, seldom regarded the wisdom of sages, and usually needed to learn the hard way. More than half my life has been spent trying to figure out whether I was supposed to be a business guy, minister, or a wanderer. Had I paid better attention to signs along the way, I believe I could have had a far more impactful life.

It turns out I'm a bit of a mutt. I'm a minister who's always been keenly interested in business yet who for the first forty years of my life dreamt about wandering. When I did pursue the Bohemian life, I discovered there are generally more nightmares than dreams-come-true. And I've learned (finally!) that having a clear sense of who I am and what I am supposed to be in this life is one of the great joys of my existence.

Reflecting on my circuitous journey there have been four basic components to finally uncovering "who I am":

1. Living a "Kierkegaard life" which is seeing life not as a problem to be solved but an adventure to be experienced.

2. Knowing that I was loved by God no matter what—as a parent loves a child—making life a freedom song that gives me confidence and an abiding sense of gratitude to God.

3. Creating opportunities to be free from the incessant noise of life through prayer, meditation, and retreat—though honestly, most often pursued through outdoor activities such as golf, windsurfing, skiing, sailing, and walking.

4. Paying attention to the times that I feel "most alive."

Advertisers, armchair philosophers, and lyricists love to write, "It's the journey, not the destination, that matters most." I get that. But for my two cents, gaining a heightened sense of who I am—*finally*, after decades of dumb ideas and relentless journeying—feels much better than one more crazy trek to find who I am supposed to be.

Ascension

Many years ago, I was close friends with a man who ran a local organization and was very active in our church. I'd stop by his office on a semi-regular basis and typically was greeted by the receptionist—a quiet woman who appeared to be in her late twenties. Our conversations were pleasant, short, and usually about less-than-arcane topics like the weather. That was the extent of our relationship.

One day when stopping in to see my friend, she looked at me in a different way that spoke of real anxiety. "May I ask you a question?" she posed. "Would you ever be willing to give me a few minutes of your time? Like after work, or something like that? I have something to share with you."

"Of course," I replied. "Is this urgent? Should we find time ASAP?"

"Oh, no" she offered. "But it is…important." We arranged to meet the following Monday.

While it is not unusual for folks outside our church to contact me to talk about any number of topics, for some reason her request felt curious—and even a little weird. The young woman appeared so anxious throughout our brief conversation that I could not help but think that something was weighing very heavily on her mind.

When I arrived at their office after work on Monday it was pouring outside—so we sat in the reception area. I sensed her anxiety was even higher than when we chatted the prior week, and so I cut to the chase.

"So, it seems like you have some important stuff on your mind," I offered. "Tell me how I can be helpful."

The young woman looked at me and proceeded to relate one of the most intense and interesting stories I'd ever heard. "First, I trust you understand that I am taking a very big risk in telling you what I am about to share. You are friends with Mr. A., and I know it is not appropriate for me to share personal things with people who come here. I have crossed the line from business to personal. And I know it could get me fired. So, I want you to know that this is not the sort of thing I usually do or have ever done before. And, I trust that you are OK with me sharing something very personal."

The prelude to her story made me both engaged and a bit nervous. I wondered if she was going to tell me about a heinous crime she had committed, that she was in a relationship with my married friend, or that she was with child and did not know what to do. I told her yes, she could trust me. She then proceeded to tell me something that blew me out of the water.

"I work here only as a way to make a living. And no one here knows any of what I am about to share with you. This work is not my life. My life is…as a child of God. I am a member of a spiritual community devoted to study and to prayer. It is how we spend most waking hours and our time on weekends. We read the Early Church Fathers, and source materials. We pray for one another, we pray for the world, and we seek to understand and fulfill God's call for us in this life."

Incredibly intrigued, and glad our conversation was spiritual in nature, I asked her how I could be of service.

"Actually," she replied, "I have thought about meeting with you for a number of weeks, but I wanted certainty that I was fulfilling God's purpose before I contacted you. This has been weighing on me, and I now know with confidence that sharing my message with you is the right thing to do. It is a message that the Spirit has placed in my heart, that you need to know."

"What is that message?" I asked amidst an intensity that made it feel as if we were the only people on the planet.

She paused, exhaled, and looked me in the eyes, offering slowly, "You may ascend in this lifetime."

I was speechless. Ascension was not part of my spiritual world. I am not sure ascension was mentioned a single time in seminary, and the only "ascension" I really knew was a Roman Catholic cemetery in the suburbs. "Ascend in this life? Help me understand what that means. Am I going to die, and you are saying I am going to heaven?" I asked, feeling a bit like a silly child talking to a mature adult.

"No," she replied. "Some people ascend while they are on this earth. It is not about dying. It is about moving to a new realm. A new spiritual place or level. You have learned lessons of the Spirit...and you may ascend. To serve the Kingdom in a new way."

Immediately, various sides of my personality kicked in. My ego appreciated what felt like a pat on the back after a lifetime of feeling that I've always fallen short spiritually. The spiritual side of my being, at least for a moment, felt moved beyond words. This woman in no way seemed looney tunes. It was apparent that she had struggled mightily with whether or not to share the message that had been placed in her heart, and it seemed almost too "out there" not to be true. I also felt a literal warmth come over me as she shared, as has happened at times when I have been in the presence of a deeply spiritual soul. I wanted to cry. I wanted to literally bow in prayer. I wanted to step deeper into the world she represented—the spiritual universe I sensed existed yet seemed so distant throughout most my life.

We talked for a few more moments as I asked about her life, and the spiritual community of which she was a part. Then I left, my mind filled with questions and ideas. "OK,

Tom, you've gotten this amazing, fresh-start message," I thought to myself, feeling like a patient whose just been told by their cardiologist that their heart is healthy, so don't screw it up now. Based on what she shared, it seemed I was good with God.

In the days that followed I fancied myself being more spiritual and reflective and Buddha-ish, you know, like I could be the "Dalai Tomah" or "Swami Tommy." And I wondered if it was all a sign that I had a higher calling beyond my local ministry. In fairly short order, though, I rarely thought about our meeting or my potential ascension. I guess it's because I think about ascension in the same way I think about heaven—that both are 100% in God's hands and that if they happen, it's only a result of God's grace. In the meantime, I have my hands full trying to make the most right here, right now, of the gift that is my life.

Within a matter of weeks following our conversation, the woman left her job and I never saw or heard from her again. It was like she was a divine double agent who disappeared after she accomplished her mission.

Maybe she was.

The Devil

In our church, you will be hard pressed to hear anything about the Devil. If you do, it's more likely to be a reference to the 2022 Duke Blue Devils Final Four basketball team than a statement about Satan. Over the years, some people have asked about my reticence to talk about—take your pick—the Devil, Satan, Beelzebub, whatever. My reasoning is pretty simple.

My job as a follower of Jesus is to seek the things he sought. I can't follow in his footsteps—that's impossible. But I can seek the things he sought, which I believe to be peace, justice, love of all, etc. Frankly, I have my hands full trying to do that.

Does it do me any good to label or identify the force—if there is such a thing—that's potentially hindering me? And if I do identify that force—*so what*? Has it gotten me any closer to my goal of seeking the things Jesus sought? No.

A football analogy is apt. If I am handed the ball and my goal is to run with it to the end zone and score a touchdown, there are two ways I can accomplish the task. The first is to run around the field, avoiding tacklers. After all, unless I run out of bounds or trip over my own two feet and fall, as long as I avoid being tackled there remains a chance I can score. The problem is, avoiding tacklers ultimately has little to do with scoring a touchdown. The goal has become avoiding being tackled, not scoring.

The other way to score is to take the handoff, fix my eyes on the goal line, disregard who's trying to tackle me, and break the plane of the goal line with the ball however I can. That is, to stay intently focused on the goal, which is scoring a touchdown.

My way of thinking about and living out my faith is not to focus on the one trying to tackle me, but instead to faithfully pursue the goal line, which is to follow the teachings of Jesus. Worrying about who or what is trying get in the way is a waste of time.

Howard Stone

Howard Stone was one of the sweetest men I've ever met. He was in his seventies when I was a young associate at the tall steepled Second Presbyterian Church in Indianapolis. He served the church as a part-time pastor, calling on the sick while also mentoring upstarts like me. Howard was a towering six feet and five inches with thick and appropriately angel-white hair.

One of my favorite Howard stories was when a group of ministers from Indianapolis went into an adult bookstore that neighbors wanted to close down. Evidently, it attracted unseemly characters and had become a major issue for many in the community. So, Howard and a half dozen other clergy went together to the store one day to confront the ownership, and to stage something of a protest.

As the story goes, when they entered the adult bookstore the other wide-eyed ministers wandered about—becoming more familiar with exactly what was for sale. Get the picture? Howard, however, was the one—loving pastor that he was—who went directly to the single employee behind the counter at the store. He introduced himself. He asked how long the employee had worked there, and what it was like to work at the store. Howard naturally cared for the man as a fellow child of God amidst the awkwardness of the situation—while the other ministers were discovering jaw-dropping photos on the covers of magazines like *Hustler* and *Truckstop Girls*.

My most unforgettable moment with Howard was when we had lunch together not long before I left Second Presbyterian. He gave me wisdom that I recall, now nearly 40 years later, quite literally every week. Howard offered, "Tom, each week when you climb into the pulpit to preach, just remember that every person, *every person*, is fighting some kind of battle."

Over the years, I have found out how right Howard was. I may know about someone's struggles, or not. Whether they are fighting for their very lives or have turned a mole hill of trivial matter into a mountain—it doesn't matter. The bottom line is that everyone is always fighting some kind of battle.

I dream what our world would be like—at home, at work, in our neighborhoods—if we remembered Howard's words: "Everyone is fighting a battle." Might we all be a bit gentler, more understanding, and not so ready to pass judgement on our sisters and brothers? Sounds nice, doesn't it?

Do You Play Backgammon?

In the summer of 1982, I served as a chaplaincy resident at a large hospital in the Chicago area. To become ordained, I had to successfully complete the program, which had a reputation for rigor and intensity. As a somewhat naive seminarian and inexperienced chaplain, I had no idea what the summer would hold—or that I'd encounter people and situations that would shape both my ministry and life.

One such experience came the very first week. As I made evening rounds late one night on my assigned floor, I noticed light spilling into the hallway from one of the patient rooms. I poked my head past the partially open door and introduced myself as the chaplain. Inside, lying on her back in bed was a woman wrapped in a blue-grey hospital-issue gown. Her name was Arianna. She had Einstein-like wiry grey hair and crooked glasses perched on the end of her nose. Tilting her head forward to look over her glasses, my introduction brought only a four-word reply: "Do you play backgammon?"

Over the next hour or so, Arianna and I got to know one another while playing midnight backgammon—something we'd do a few times in the weeks that would follow. I learned a lot about Arianna that night as she shared stories about her life, children, and work. I learned about all she'd done during her full but often challenging life. As importantly, in the weeks that followed I also learned what she'd not done or thought about during her 50+ years.

You see, Arianna had never given much thought to what she believed, thought, or felt about God. She'd attended a Greek Orthodox Church as a child, and at one stage delved into Rosicrucianism, which she discovered through a small, square ad in the back of a magazine. But as an adult Arianna had never really come to a place of peace on what she thought or felt about God, or her own mortality.

That all changed when after two frustrating weeks of tests Arianna received her diagnosis: colon cancer. In the days that followed, in what would be the final moments of her life, Arianna scrambled. Her initial response to the cancer would have made Positive Mental Attitude Guru W. Clement Stone proud. She wrote letters to herself, and to her cancerous colon, which she taped to the walls in her room and bathroom. Arianna declared in the letters that she'd not accept the cancer in her body—and ordered it to be banished all together.

Following the letters came one of the most curious requests I'd ever received. One morning while stopping by to check her spirits and see if she was up for a game of backgammon, Arianna asked me to "magnetize her water." She explained that she'd purposely kept a closed, deep violet-blue glass vase sitting by the window for a few days so that it would absorb positive rays from the sun. Arianna told me that I could enhance the water further by holding the blue vase in the sunlight in such a way that allowed for my thumbs to touch, side-by-side. My personal energy would combine with the energy of the sun to "magnetize the water"—giving it unique power. She believed, or *hoped*, that as she drank the magnetized water the cancer consuming her body would be overpowered and flushed from her system.

Before you judge Arianna as being nuttier than a fruitcake, keep in mind that she had been diagnosed with a life-threatening form of cancer and that she was also pursuing every traditional means of treatment possible. She was a woman who loved her children and was passionate about life. Arianna was desperate to do anything, everything that could possibly help her live.

In what would be the final two weeks of her life, most of which were spent in the oncology unit, Arianna continued to scramble. She tried anything and everything to hang on to her life. She asked me about my faith and the way of Jesus, and at her request, we prayed together. Then one day she requested that I join her and her family the next evening for a special gathering in her hospital room, as they'd made arrangements for a Pentecostal faith healer from the south side of Chicago to offer a special healing service at her bedside.

The next night the faith healer—a woman barely five feet tall clad in what appeared to be the full, black habit of a nun—came to Arianna's private room. Arianna was drained and her "how 'bout a game of backgammon" spunk and energy had left. Cancer had taken its toll and it seemed certain that she was on death's door.

Of course, this did not deter the passionate faith healer. She introduced herself to the family, then asked who I was—but only after reminding the family that she had requested no one outside the family be permitted in the room. Arianna said, "Tom stays," and the faith healer paused, but then nodded in agreement before stepping from the room. Five minutes later the healer returned only to say, "Tonight is not right. The spirits are not here. I will come back tomorrow. The same time." As she left, no one knew what to say.

The next night the faith healer returned dressed in a white robe, like a nun's habit, only this time with an assistant. They placed and lit a variety of candles throughout the room and turned off the lights. It felt like what I'd imagined a séance would be—both eerie and exciting. The candles cast an orange glow in the room as the faith healer talked to God, calling upon divine spirits. She began to speak in tongues. Passion poured from her being with each word she spoke, and tears flowed down the cheeks of Arianna's one adult and two college-aged children.

The faith healer told us all to close our eyes as she turned up the volume, almost yelling as she implored God to heal what she called the "evil spirits and demons" within Arianna. Then, placing her hands on her head she told Arianna, who had been flat on her back and unable to move for days, to sit up. I couldn't help but peek out my left eye to watch what followed. Amidst the ghostly darkness accented only by flickering candles, Arianna rather miraculously moved forward to sit up, her wide eyes reflecting both energy and terror. But what I also noticed was Arianna being pulled forward to her upright position by the faith healer with what remained of Arianna's thin, Einstein hair.

Then the faith healer with deep conviction proclaimed Arianna "healed" as her children opened their teary eyes to find their mother sitting up in bed. Arianna was in an ecstatic state and began to gently sing a song she'd sung as a little girl. It was an incredible moment of mind-boggling ambiguity. I'd just witnessed what I felt was both abuse and fraud by the faith healer, yet what followed was a moment of transcendent peace as Arianna sang in angelic whispers.

Arianna soon came out of her trance-like place and was eased down so she could lie flat. Then, to my great surprise, she asked everyone—from the faith healer to her three children—to leave the room. "Except for Tom," she whispered. We'd come along ways since she our first backgammon game. Her oldest daughter hesitated, stating she wanted to remain. Arianna's lack of response indicated her desires, and her daughter left the room, quietly closing the door behind her.

I stepped forward to stand alongside her bed, my hands resting on the safety rail. Leaning forward to within a foot of her face and looking into her glassy, unfocused eyes, I said a quick, silent prayer, "Oh God, what do I say?"

Arianna then spoke in a voice mixed with uncertainty, hope, and exhaustion. "Tom...am I healed?" Surprisingly, as if God had heard my prayer, words came instantly in response, though in retrospect their ambiguity makes it seem as if I had attended years of law school, not seminary. "If you believe you are healed, then you are," I whispered.

Two days later, Arianna died.

* * * * *

During my summer as a Chaplain, I developed relationships with scores of patients, a several who died while in the hospital. For some who passed, as with Arianna, the final moments of their earthly lives were marked by an intense effort to "figure everything out."

"Is there a God?"

"Does God care?"

"Will God help me if I pray?"

"What happens when I die?"

"Is there a heaven and an afterlife?"

"Is eternal life only for people who believe in God?"

"Will I go to hell because I've not been a believer?"

"What does faith mean for me in life—and in death?"

For these people, the end of life became a kind of earthly hell almost entirely devoid of peace.

Yet I also spent time with people who had previously wrestled with the key questions of life and death during their time on this earth. They weren't all Christians and represented many ways of knowing and experiencing God. For them, the final moments of their lives yielded a deep peace marked by gratitude and even joy—making their transition to new life a profound, spiritual moment of the highest order.

What's the point? The point of sharing Arianna's story is not to encourage you to pursue faith as some sort of "eternal life insurance policy," but to remind you that we do ourselves a monumental disservice if during our lives, we do not come to a place of reasonable comfort with life's key questions. In part, that is what inspires this book and my ministry.

But what also inspires my writing is what I've witnessed over nearly 40 years in ministry. That while it is important to consider life's key questions for the sake of our deaths, it is even more important to consider them for the sake of our lives—right here, right now.

Serendipity

Serendipity is defined as "finding agreeable, beneficial, or positive things not sought." Frankly, there's more serendipity in my life than I deserve. One serendipitous moment was when I was trying to affect the turn-around of the struggling Union Church of Lake Bluff. Before I arrived, the congregation had plummeted from 200 members to 66 in five years, in part due to a fight over a pipe organ. Sounds like just the sort of thing churches get into, right? And the struggle to stay afloat was so significant that they'd even formed a task force to consider how to properly dispose of the church building and assets (though no one told me this until *after* I accepted the job).

It turns out I was very fortunate to be called as the church's minister, and in many ways, it was perfect place for me at the time. The church leaders—exhausted after years of laboring to hold the congregation together—gave me the freedom to "sing my own song," which was generally not possible in the large, institutional church I had previously served.

One of the challenges, though, was that they did not have the financial resources for me to make much of a living, and I received no health or retirement benefits. And, while I loved the church, I also remained intrigued with getting back into the business world part time both because I enjoyed business and could use the money. So, I crafted a plan with my sister Sue to create a boutique corporate training firm that would take advantage of her human resources skills and connections and my abilities as a speaker and facilitator.

One day a man named Jack who was brand new to our church came to our 6:30 am prayer group. Jack stayed after our prayers finished and we chatted to get to know one another. He was quite engaging, and for some unknown reason I felt comfortable sharing this new idea about the corporate training firm that my sister Sue and I were going to launch.

After I finished sharing our vision, the charismatic Jack looked me in the eye with a smile and asked, "Why do that?"

I replied "I'm not sure what you mean…"

"Why start your own company—when you can come to work for me?"

"Huh? What do you do?"

"I have a corporate training business," said Jack with a characteristically broad smile. "And I need a guy just like you."

The next week I began part-time work as an independent contractor at Jack's company. For several years, it provided me the opportunity to work a day here and a day there in a way that fit my church schedule, to travel, to supplement my income, and to be engaged with the business world that I so enjoyed.

That's serendipity. An undeserved blessing that came my way. The $64,000 question, of course, was God's hand somehow involved in the great blessing I received? Was Spirit driving the exchange between Jack and me that ultimately helped make it possible for me to fulfill an important life vision? Is that how God works in the world today?

I haven't a clue.

To some, I'm sure my response reflects a faith that is lackluster and disappointing, particularly when we look to our ministers, priests, and rabbis for confident answers regarding God—not "I haven't a clue." I genuinely wish I had greater clarity and insight. The truth is that for 50 years I've had extraordinarily powerful spiritual experiences, rich blessings, and moments when I sensed active divine presence. And, for 50 years I've also had times when it felt like God was AWOL and nowhere to be found.

While I live confident that God is at work in the world today, I do not begin to know either how or when. That's the place I find myself amidst my constantly evolving faith. For me, faith is not about living in God's world with a certainty that leaves no room for questions but living in God's world amidst uncertainty—yet still daring to trust God. It's not a faith that is for everyone, but at the end of the day it is honest. And for faith to be meaningful, it must be honest.

Garage Sale Buddha

Joyful Wonder

About 15 years ago, it became clear the Community Church really needed an office. For our first five years, I used the cabin of my sailboat *Anam Cara* as my workspace from April 1 through October 31. It was awesome for quiet work, but because it was in a harbor twenty minutes north of our town it was less than ideal for meetings—and only available seven months during the year. The local Starbucks was okay, but not so good for the occasionally intense one-on-one meeting. And, while I never minded working out of my Mini Cooper, it was a bit snug. As for our basement where I had a desk, my books and had desperately tried to create an office? I couldn't stand it. I hated the basement no matter how creatively I dressed up the concrete walls or what cool stuff I hung from the cobwebbed pipes. More than anything, I needed a place to meet with people. It was time to find an office.

I looked at commercial space in downtown Lake Forest and Lake Bluff and considered renting a room or studio office. Nothing seemed right until I walked past a tiny little two-story building in Lake Bluff. It was surrounded by weeds and, even though I had lived in town for over fifteen years, the building was so skinny that I had barely noticed it. I looked in the window and saw a random chair and desk that appeared to not be in use.

I asked my friend and local realtor Brad Andersen who owned the building and he shared it was Doug Karnazes, the guy who ran Bluffington's Café, the sandwich shop next-door. I had never met Doug, and so I went in and introduced myself and asked him if he did, indeed, own the building.

Doug told me that he was the owner, and when I asked if he was interested in renting, Doug took off his apron and we went next door. He gave me a tour of the building, which was basically two rooms that were sixteen feet by sixteen feet, a balcony, and a restroom just a little bigger than your average jetliner lavatory.

Following the two-minute tour, I asked Doug "What do you want for it?"

"What would you offer?" Doug asked.

I said, "How about $1,000 a month?"

Doug agreed, we shook hands, and everything was perfect. It all happened that quickly.

In the years that followed, we fixed up the tired space and landscaping, and in another handshake deal, Doug agreed to not raise our rent as long as we continued to improve the property. We could not have had a better landlord, and Doug promised if anyone ever wanted to buy the office or if he needed to sell it, that we'd have the first option to purchase it.

One day, after eight years renting the building, Doug came to the office and said in his usual friendly, but matter-of-fact way, "Tommy, I need to talk to you. Someone wants to buy the building. They want to give me $400,000 for it. So, Tommy, I told the guy that I needed to give you the first option. You've got a week. Let me know."

And he walked out.

My jaw dropped, and my heart sank. I could not believe that anyone would actually pay $400,000 for a two-room office building with a worthless balcony and a tiny half bath in little downtown Lake Bluff, Illinois. $400,000 was *twice* our annual budget.

Topping it off, it all occurred during the summer—our financially quietest time of the year—when we didn't have more than $8,000 liquid assets. We also had no real savings, so the thought of suddenly coming up with $400,000 was pretty crazy.

I spent the next four days—Wednesday through Saturday—considering every possible option in Lake Forest and Lake Bluff. There were no viable possibilities. Everything was too expensive, and nothing gave us the visibility of our tiny but perfectly located building in downtown Lake Bluff. And, though there were some places on the second floor of local office buildings, they just didn't feel right for our wonderful, bright, and open office—which I had enhanced by building an outdoor patio affectionately called "The Pastoral Beer Garden." It was not looking good with just a couple of days to go.

That Saturday night at about 10:00 pm it occurred to me that I needed to say something to our congregation the next morning. I spent the following two hours drafting a ten-minute statement—believing that people in the church needed to know what was about to happen to our much-loved "world headquarters".

At Worship on the Beach the next morning, I told those gathered that what was happening was "sort of like a Harvard Business School versus Harvard Divinity School case study."

"Now, I'm basically a free market guy," I said, "and believe if someone has the money to come along and purchase a building then they ought to be able to do that." But I explained there was another side to me that was pretty bummed out because I was fairly confident the person seeking to buy the building had numerous options that we simply did not. I surmised there were at least a few buildings he could purchase in the area. I suppose I sounded a little whiny at the beach that morning, but I needed to make the point—we were about to lose a very important and precious asset in our ministry, one that we could not readily replace. After sharing the story several people expressed concern, but that was about it. We were one day closer to losing our office.

The next morning, I received a phone call from the executive assistant of a gentleman who for the very first time had attended church the prior day with his family. She inquired if I had time to stop by his office for a visit that day. I told her I'd be happy to come and arranged to meet him after lunch.

I did not know the man who prefers to remain anonymous, but I knew of him and was intrigued by his desire to meet with me. Potentially, a wonderful family for our church, I thought, which did turn out to be the case. But something else very special happened at that meeting.

Walking into his spartan office, we shook hands and exchanged small talk for a few moments before he said, "You know I don't really know you, but it seems like you're trying to do some good things. I'd like to try and help. So, here's what I'll do. I'll give you a matching grant to help buy the building. Whatever amount you want up to $100,000. If you want $30,000, I'll give you $30,000. And if you want $100,000, I'll give you a $100,000. But, in order to get money from me you have to raise at least as much as you say you want. So, if you tell me you want me to give you $100,000 but you only raise $99,000 from other people, I'm not giving you a penny. You have to raise what you say you are going to raise. What do you think?"

"Fantastic, it sounds fantastic. Thank you," I answered, a bit overwhelmed at our good fortune.

"So, how much do you think you want?"

Without even a hint of hesitation I replied, "$100,000," as our generous, anonymous donor smiled at my moxie. I was not about to leave a penny on the table!

As I left his office that day, I was nothing short of blown away. What are the odds that someone would come to church—a church that had been in existence for over 10 years—for the first time ever on the day I make a rather desperate plea for us to keep our office space? What are the odds not only that the new person would not be turned off, but be inspired and also have the financial resources to offer us a $100,000 gift? And then—to actually do so? It was unbelievable.

The next week I sent out a letter to people in our congregation sharing the good news and asking for support to match the $100,000. I did that after a memorable meeting with Doug—to tell him that we absolutely did want to buy the building!

Doug was amazed, I was amazed, and everyone I knew was amazed. From out of nowhere came a true hero in the nick of time.

Within a couple weeks we raised $115,000. Combined with the generous donor's gift, the $215,000 allowed us to make a nice down payment on the $400,000 building, which ultimately gave us a lower mortgage payment then our previous monthly rent payments. And, probably most importantly, we gained control over the destiny of our little two-room office.

In the end, it's the story of a great blessing coming to the Community Church. And while I hesitate to spiritualize a real estate transaction, the story of a stranger coming to church for the first time on a day of great need in the history of the church and within 24 hours offering us $100,000 is, well, mind blowing. However, I don't feel a need to point toward God as if the unlikely experience was given to us as some sort of evidence of the divine. I'm absolutely content being filled with a sense of joyful wonder.

Blessed Beyond Measure

Shortly after renting our Lake Bluff office building, my good friends and church folks David and Patty Ritter and I talked about how ugly the office landscaping was—and how nice it would be to make a change. David and Patsy are master gardeners, and well-known in our community for their breath-taking and creatively landscaped yard at their former home across the street from Lake Michigan.

Not surprisingly, one day David came by with a few tools and started digging up some of the stringy, invasive weeds that dominated the area surrounding the building. Pretty soon, everything was torn apart, with piles of weeds, dead bushes, branches, and dirt everywhere. The problem was that we needed to do something other than just remove the weeds.

So, David and Patsy put together a beautiful landscape plan which included a hardscape, new walkway, trees, and bushes that would dramatically change the entire look of the building and beautify an important corner in downtown Lake Bluff. The only problem? The *usual* problem—"How do we pay for it?" Of course, we had next to no money. And whether cluelessly, carelessly, or faithfully, I don't know—we just moved forward and assumed it would all work out and the money would turn up.

Exacerbating the problem just a bit is the fact is that David and Patsy—while always sensitive to costs—also always do things in a first-class way. When I asked David and Patsy what their beautiful plan would cost, they estimated the total cost for everything to be about $9,000. To have a professional landscape architectural firm come up with the design and implementation would almost certainly be three times that. For whatever reason, I wasn't worried about finding the money, though in retrospect I should have been and can't believe I was quite so clueless.

Then, about 10 days into the landscaping project as David, Patsy, Perry Walcott, and others implemented the Ritters' design, Sue Nelson called me. "Tom, I see you are doing something at the church office. What's going on?"

"Well, the small area around the church office is so ugly—we're doing everything we can to make it look good for the church and the community," I replied. "It's an eyesore, and David and Patsy Ritter have created a beautiful landscape plan."

"Well, Tom, here's what I'd like to do," Sue said. "I'd like you to let me pay for it. My husband Ben always wanted to make downtown Lake Bluff look as nice as it possibly could, so you tell me how much money you need, and I'll take care of it."

"Wow. Amazing," I said, filled with elation. "But, Sue, to be honest it's going to be about $9,000 or $10,000 by the time it's all said and done."

"No problem, Tom. Just tell me the number when you're done, and I'll drop a check off."

It's experiences like this that inspired a phrase that I have found myself using regularly around the Community Church the last 15 years—blessed beyond measure. Simply put, we've been way more fortunate than what we deserve. Blessed beyond measure.

The Deal

The Lily Reed Holt Memorial Chapel at Lake Forest College, listed on the National Historic Register and complete with original Tiffany windows and lamps, is a perfect spot for our services. We've worshiped there each year from September through May since our first service in 1999, and the acoustics for our musically oriented church are very good. The last thing we ever wanted to do was lose the privilege of meeting in the Chapel.

So, after years of waiting for just the right moment, I approached the Vice President of Business, the late Leslie Chapman, with a proposal. We'd give the College $25,000 cash upfront—in addition to our rent—if they would extend our contract for Sunday morning in the Chapel for seventeen years. Basically, it would ensure our use of the Chapel even beyond the time that I would likely still be at the church. And it would give the College a heightened profile in the community by bringing 100 to 200 people to campus each week, and an annually increasing revenue stream for an extended period for a space that was never used on Sunday mornings. A great deal for all!

Of course, you guessed the problem—I made a promise that we would come up with $25,000—without having any idea of where the $25,000 might come from. When Leslie agreed to the deal, I excitedly sent an email to the six Monkey Boys (the folks who kept an eye on church finances) to tell them of the wonderful news, as well as to share our challenge—where would we come up with $25,000?

Over the next few hours, I received a number of replies, all of which were encouraging—but none which offered advice as to where we might come up with what was then about 15% of our annual budget.

The next morning, arriving at the church office I noticed an envelope on the floor by the mail slot at the base of the door. I opened it up. It was a check for $25,000 from one of the Monkey Boys. Unbelievable, extreme generosity once again, and God seemingly at work once again. Not in a breathtaking, miraculous manner, but instead through a very generous person who was inspired to help us continue to do God's work on Sunday mornings in the Chapel.

A Reluctant Evangelist

Truth be told, despite having been active in the church world for half a century and spending most Sundays the last 30 years standing in front of people at worship services talking about God, I am at best a reluctant evangelist. Telling people they *have* to believe or *exactly how* they should believe in God just doesn't feel right, any more than telling someone how they should grill a steak or what color to paint their house. And I'm not too big, either, on the word "believe." I prefer "trust," but that's a topic for another time.

Maybe I was turned off while I was a high school student listening to the impassioned pleas of arm-twisting believers who made it seem like I was an idiot if I didn't believe. Or, possibly, I've just become sickened one time too many watching fervent and, in some cases, totally corrupt televangelists exclaim "Praise the Lord!" though they mostly wanted people to "Pass the Cash."

Today, at the Community Church of Lake Forest and Lake Bluff where I preach most Sundays, my goal is not to get people to follow a certain belief model, but to feed people and inspire their connection with God to experience an authentic, meaning-filled faith that makes a difference in their lives and our world.

Maybe the best way to characterize this is by recalling a television ad from the 1970s. A mechanic is shown standing in a garage, in front of a car up on a hoist. In his hand, the mechanic holds a Fram oil-filter up and says, "You can pay me now...or pay me later." The point? Like it or not, taking care of the engine is something that you will need to do sooner or later, and it's probably wise to do now.

So it is with the great questions of life and faith. I am less the fervent evangelist and more the mechanic reminding folks that virtually all of us will have to address those questions at some stage. What remains uncertain is whether it will be in a frantic manner as was the case with Arianna, or whether we will take the opportunity to consider the questions *before* we have no choice.

I may be a reluctant evangelist, but I hope with all my heart you'll take an opportunity to consider those questions sooner rather than later. In doing so, I believe that it will make a difference not just in *how you think about* life and death, but *how you live* each and every day.

Work

Preaching in Northwestern University garb one Sunday
after losing a bet to my friend, passionate NU alum Jay Sharman

Garage Sale Buddha

Work Harder, Not Smarter

I knew I'd get your attention. Everyone always says, "work smarter, not harder." I love that saying, but the only problem is that working smarter is not always possible, especially if you're not the sharpest knife in the drawer. That's me. Not sure why, but some people (not everyone!) think I'm brighter than I am.

A joke I've used when speaking to educational groups is that "I graduated in the top 10% of my high school class...the top 10% of *the bottom third.*" It gets a laugh, but it's true. Since 3rd or 4th grade, I've been a rather poor student. Sitting in class was truly painful. On top of it, while I enjoy reading, I turn the pages at a sloth-like pace— painfully slow. You get the picture. I've never been Ivy League material, though because I am an OK communicator, I'm generally perceived by most as being smarter than I probably am.

Now, while I always endeavor to work smarter, since I am *not smarter*, it doesn't always work. (If you are shaking your head saying "Hey, I'm not sure that makes sense," I've just proven my point. I'm not that smart.)

So, I'm probably just smart enough, at best. That means that I, along with millions of other people like me, have no choice but to work harder if we want to get ahead.

A couple of experiences have confirmed this. Many years ago, another minister in town who'd heard about the success of our Worship on the Beach services decided that she'd bring her congregation down to the shores of Lake Michigan for a service. She and her team had the experience of spending early Sunday morning cleaning the open-air shelter followed by lugging chairs and tables and musical equipment and coffee and everything else needed for worship down the bluff to the shelter. Then it all needed to be set up—only to be taken down 90 minutes later after the service and hauled up the hill to be put away back at the church. The less-than-pleasant weather made it even worse for my friend.

The next week when we saw each other I asked about her experience worshiping on the beach. She winced with pursed lips and shook her head and asked, "You really do that every week?"

"Yup."

"You've got to be crazy. We're *never* doing that again." She's probably right about the crazy part, or at least that I am crazy enough to know that I need to work harder if I want to get ahead. You see, there's an option if you are not Albert Einstein—work harder, and most times you can more than make up for not being Phi Beta Kappa material.

The other example is when after ten years, our church decided to stop hosting the Fourth of July Family Fair for our town. We'd created the event in the very early years of the church (a classic exercise in affiliated marketing) and it blossomed to the place where our town park was filled with happy kids and families for three and a half hours every Fourth of July after the legendary town parade. Tons of goodwill, and we typically cleared $15,000. Not bad for an event that ran for less than four hours.

After 10 years, our devoted volunteers were running out of gas. My friend Penny Marsh jokingly began to call it the "Community Church Not-So-Fun Family Fair." I heard Penny and others loud and clear, so after our final Family Fair we packed the games and tents and prizes and stuff up and put it all in our Metro Storage site.

In the months that followed, I approached people affiliated with not-for-profits in town—Scouts, school groups, etc.—and made an offer: We'd give them everything they needed to run the Fair, including an extraordinary book prepared by our volunteer leader Nancy Considine Clark that detailed how to run every game, where to order the prizes, etc. We'd even loan any group that took over the Fair the ten tents that we used to run the event and give them a few thousand dollars in prizes.

Now, given how many cookies Girl Scouts must sell to make a buck, and the amount of uber-expensive popcorn the Cub Scouts need to move to pay for their program, I thought someone would jump at the chance to net $15,000 in part of an afternoon. Not to mention the goodwill and visibility they'd receive by hosting a high-profile event on the most beloved day of the year in our town.

To my great surprise and disappointment, not a single group—*not one*—was interested in taking over the Family Fair and the $15,000 or more they could pocket. Why? Their universal response was "getting all those volunteers (125+) together on the Fourth of July? No way! Too much work!"

The reward was there, just waiting for a taker. But no one was willing to do the work, even when the most challenging task of creating a successful event from scratch had already been done. The bottom line? Work smarter if that's an option, but *everyone* can always work harder.

Garage Sale Buddha

What's the Need?

Go online and Google "business failures" and you'll see an amazing array of baffling products and services. Here are just a few ideas that fell flat on their faces, in some cases costing investors tens of millions of dollars:

1. Jimmy Dean Chocolate Chip Pancakes and Sausage on a Stick.
2. MyFuneral.com, a service to help you pick a DJ for your funeral.
3. The iSmell usb that emits an odor from your computer when you get an email.
4. Homeless Tours, where for $2,000 you get to spend a few days with people who are homeless.

The truth is you probably don't have to look any farther than your own community to find a business failure, like your neighbor who was absolutely convinced that they could start a podcast or blog or YouTube channel that would yield big bucks swiftly. According to the Bureau of Labor Statistics, 20% of small businesses fail in their first year, 30% of small business fail in their second year, and 50% of small businesses fail after five years. Ultimately, 70% of small business owners fail by their tenth year in business. What separates those who have sustainable success from those that fade away? More than anything, *meeting an ongoing need.*

If you are starting a business or a church or any kind of organization, before you do anything else, make sure you are meeting an existing need. Because I've started a few things that have worked out over the years (and some that have failed), I'm sometimes asked my opinion about new business ideas. My first question is always "What need or needs are you going to meet?" Followed by "What unique capacity do you have to meet those needs?" Then, we drill deeper into areas like "Who is your competition?" and "What is your niche, and the position you intend to claim in the marketplace?"

In the end, though, it is *all* about meeting needs.

The Community Church works for a variety of reasons, many of which have nothing to do with me. Generous and trusting congregants. Serendipitous / spiritual blessings I cannot explain. Spectacular music. Great co-workers. Cool places to worship. However, the one thing I did do that got the whole ball rolling was bet the farm that there was a need twitching to be met on the North Shore of Chicago for a spiritually progressive, open-minded faith community.

Think about your business or organization. What is the need you are meeting in the eyes of the population you serve? And, if you are up and running after three or five or seven years and beginning to struggle, ask yourself if the needs you endeavor to meet are the same as when you began, and if your focus has switched from customer needs...to your needs.

I'm sure I make my Community Church co-workers crazy because of this, but I always get suspicious when we fine-tune our processes to make life and work easier for us. To stay in business, whether a church or a local grocery store, you must stay passionately focused on the needs of your customers...not your needs.

Organic Marketing

I may be a minister, but deep down inside I'm also a sales and marketing guy. I've sold everything from dental pharmaceuticals and heavy-duty truck parts to menswear. I've offered sales seminars to companies throughout the United States and Canada. I created and directed a marketing and communications department at a liberal arts college, and the focus of my doctoral thesis was on marketing for non-profit organizations. To me, marketing—all the ways you increase the likelihood you'll connect with the kind of customers you seek—has always been the fun stuff about business.

Yet despite my interests and background, in recent years I've spent very little time focused on marketing our church. Why? It's because the Community Church benefits from the most effective marketing out there—*organic marketing*. We've evolved to become this marketing guy's dream—our "customers" come to us guided primarily by word-of-mouth.

What's the ticket to organic marketing, where your customers naturally do the work for you? It may be one of the greatest business lessons I've learned: organic marketing is the result of offering consistent, high-quality experiences for your customers. As one speaker shared in a class many years ago, "If you want to improve your marketing, improve your service." She was right.

In the early days of our church, I spent exorbitant amounts of time and energy making what I thought were all the right marketing moves. Establishing a solid web site. Choosing a memorable name. Finding a niche. Creating a position. Getting a dynamic logo that differentiated us. Affiliating the church alongside known and respected community organizations. They were the right things to do, back in 1999.

We marketed ourselves as aggressively as our tiny budget would allow. Yet we continued to struggle, as reflected in the church's financial profile during our first three years—never taking in more than $24,000 in a single year. From that paltry revenue, we had to pay for rent, musicians, insurance, marketing, computers, internet, etc. Folks just weren't showing up. I sometimes told people, "Our Sunday worship attendance is like a football game—about eleven on each side."

Then we made a few changes, including jettisoning our ambiguous "Community Worship Hour" name to become "the Community Church." We decided to forgo worshiping on Saturdays at 5:00 p.m. in favor of the traditional Sunday service time at 10:00 a.m. And, as attendance grew, in the first year we nearly doubled our revenue from prior years.

What was the change that mattered most? It had nothing to do with strategy or marketing. Instead, it was when a very talented, well-connected, sweet-in-the-best-sense-of-the-word guy named Ken Hall joined us as Music Director. Ken made certain that we had inspiring music each Sunday. Gone were the days of my playing an inarguably pedestrian "Kum Bah Yah," or stretching my music creativity to the max by singing "Amazing Grace" to the tune of the Animal's "House of the Rising Sun." As we began to offer a consistently higher quality worship experience, people began to invite their friends without fear that they'd have to apologize for a dismal service. Instead, they could invite friends confident that they'd have a positive experience.

Marketing matters. Names, logos, advertising, websites, social media—they all matter. But what has been demonstrated time and again in all kinds of organizations and yes, even churches like ours, is that there is no marketing more important than organic marketing—which is neither a process or a goal, but the result of offering a consistently high-quality service or product. At the Community Church, it turned out that one of the best marketing moves we ever made was actually a personnel decision when we hired Ken Hall because it increased the quality of our worship experience.

Wanting to expand your business or grow your organization? Consider for a few moments setting aside time-consuming social media programs, websites, advertising and what you *think* drives your success, and ask, "how can we improve what we do for our customers and clients?"

Garage Sale Buddha

Forget About Growth

Many years ago, I served as the President of our local Rotary Club. During my tenure, I ran the club pretty much like I run the church—my focus was on having an engaging weekly experience that fed Rotarians more than just bacon at each Wednesday breakfast. As with the church, we enjoyed our time together and managed to do some good things along the way. While I respected the work of Rotary International, I'll admit I spent very little time as President participating in regional, District events and programs. For me, 90% of my time as President was focused on our local Club.

At the end of my tenure, I was notified by the District that we had won an award as the Chicago-area club that had grown the most during the year. As a result, they asked if I would lead a session at the Annual District 6440 Conference and share my "secrets" on growth. Knowing that many Rotary Clubs were struggling in our *Bowling Alone* culture where voluntary associations of every kind were dying, I said yes.

However, in the interest of transparency I told them that not only did the Lake Forest / Lake Bluff Morning Rotary Club have no growth strategy, but that we "consciously avoided talking about Club growth." Evidently desperate for a speaker, they encouraged me to make a presentation nonetheless, so I agreed.

When it came time for the session, I stood before about 30 or 40 devoted (and in some cases desperate) Rotarians in a session the District titled "How to Grow Your Rotary Club." I shared:

1. Our club had no growth strategy.
2. We never talked about growing the club.

3.   My firm belief that growth is a result, not a goal.

As I let my initial words sink in, the group sat silent. I think they were dumbfounded and wondering if they were either (a) on Candid Camera or (b) if I was the jerk I appeared to be—and *not that funny*. As they represented Clubs struggling to stay afloat let alone grow, I imagine I came across as completely aloof.

I stuck with it, though, and drilled down to try and get them to understand what I was saying beyond my baffling initial three points.

"How would you feel if you were not in a club," I asked "and a Rotarian told you that they wanted you to join? You'd probably feel a bit flattered—but only until you found out that the club was struggling to stay afloat and that they really needed new members badly. Then you'd feel like you were not the special person they wanted in the club because of who you are. Instead, you'd feel like you were the object of their institutional desperation to stay afloat. They wanted you not so much for you, as for them. How does that feel?"

Most seemed to get where I was going as I made the point that the focus should be on creating a Rotary Club and experience that meets people's needs so that they want to join—and not making people the object of institutional goals.

Then to emphasize one of the few things in life that I am absolutely 100% confident about, I elaborated on my belief, "growth is a result, not a goal."

"Our Club philosophy, at least on my watch," I offered, "begins with the Rotarian, not the Club. The job of the Club is to get inside the lives of the people who show up each week—or new folks who might—and understand what would provide value in their lives that was in sync with Rotary's stated goals. What would get them out of bed *every*

Wednesday for breakfast by 7:15 a.m.? The answers were pretty simple for the entire club:

1. An enjoyable time.
2. Breakfast with plenty of bacon.
3. Opportunities to connect with others.
4. The chance to participate in some good works.
5. An enjoyable time.

I purposely re-emphasized the enjoyable time—because breakfast, business and social connections, and good works were not enough for most without it also being an enjoyable time. And if someone doesn't *want* to enjoy themselves, they're probably not who you want in the Club. We created opportunities for the people in our Club to start their day with a smile.

So, it doesn't matter if you are in a local Rotary Club or a church, run a restaurant or sell sterile gauze sponges for a living. Forget about growth as a goal, which turns your customers / clients / congregants / club members into objects. Instead, think of growth as the result of doing the right things for the right reasons, and meeting needs in sync with your core values.

Garage Sale Buddha

Multiple Yesses

Back in the early days of our church, I often wondered why more people didn't join us. Part of it had to do with our ineffectiveness in meeting people's needs.

For example, we met at a difficult time. Worship quality was inconsistent. People did not come to our services confident they would have a high-quality liturgical experience. As a preacher, I was uneven at best, and often exhausted while trying to be a husband, father, provider, and new church guy. The music director the first three years Jon Nordgren, while a spirited and gifted musician, was also a full-time firefighter whose schedule only allowed him to be there—at most—two weeks out of three.

In short, there weren't many reasons to say "yes" to what we then called "The Community Worship Hour."

Over the course of 20 years, though, we've gotten over the hump and have gone from being just an idea to having roughly 350 families consider us as their church home. I am convinced that, in addition to providing more consistent quality at our services, we've grown in direct result to the additional reasons we've provided for people to say "yes" to the Community Church.

For a while, the one reason people said "yes" to coming to the Community Worship Hour was to *maybe* hear a stirring message or tune—or because they were friends and felt bad no one was showing up. And not many came.

But then Ken Hall joined us and there was another reason people said "yes" to becoming part of us—to enjoy the inspiring music he put in place each week. Then we started holding a third of our services each year on the shores of Lake Michigan, which became a super-appealing reason for many to say "yes".

Over time the list of why people say "yes" to our church has grown. We developed a unique program in Africa that became a separate charity called KidsUganda. During his tenure with us, the affable Rev. Zachary Hancock helped move young families and meditation devotees to say "yes." Today, Rev. Sean Miller's outstanding study groups and compelling sermons inspire people to "yes." The list goes on—our unique Roots and Wings Sunday School, Kate Cole's Sunday nursery that's positioned as "playgroup" for young children, and fellowship events that range from Bocce Ball Tournaments to an Annual Christmas Party where we rent out the local Micro Brewery, to our yearly beach picnic.

There's a correlation between growth and the number of reasons that people are inspired to say "yes." What are the reasons people say "yes" to your organization, business… or you?

Get the Show on the Road

The other night I attended the Gardener's Book Club. Looking at the dozen participants gathered around the dining table, there appeared to be no diversity, whatsoever. Everyone was male, white and, in broad terms, successful. Yet what made the evening wonderful was because the participants—all bright—didn't necessarily view the world in the same way. In fact, on this evening when Nebraska Senator Ben Sasse's *THEM* was our topic of discussion, the group had spirited and far-reaching conversations that reflected significant philosophical differences.

By the evening's end we were seriously off topic—that happens—and found ourselves discussing our local faith communities. In recent years a few of the churches in town have had a challenge transitioning to new pastoral leadership. Many parishioners and congregants have been frustrated, finding it understandably ridiculous to take two or more years to find new senior church leadership. Mind you, it's often more a denominational than a local issue, but the fact remained that it seemed to take forever to get a new Pastor or Priest—and upsetting parishioners no end. In short, it took a lot of the wind of out of a few local church's sails.

A fairly new friend, Bill, who attends the Community Church periodically and was at the Gardener's Book Club, put the whole matter wonderfully in perspective in his quiet way when he offered "I don't get why it takes two or three years to find a new minister or priest. Didn't Jesus do his entire ministry in three years?"

What a great point, Bill. What's taking too long in your life or organization? Get the show on the road! After all, Jesus changed the world in just three years—and we're still talking about him 2000 years later.

Garage Sale Buddha

Mission Statements

Businesses and churches and organizations of all kinds have this thing for mission statements. I'll admit that I don't get it. All too often, creating a mission statement is an exhausting exercise in bureaucratic and political correctness where an unbelievable amount of time is spent arguing about minutiae. Then, after the statement is finished and published everyone feels great...but mostly because they are through with a very tedious and onerous task. Unfortunately, mission statements are often then put in a drawer and forgotten, until a new leader comes along and claims it's time for a new mission statement.

Rare is the organization that allows their mission statement to be a meaningful guide informing how they go about their business. However, there are some who seem to, such as Patagonia:

Build the best product, cause no unnecessary harm, use business to inspire and implement solutions to the environmental crisis.

Or, World Bicycle Relief:

World Bicycle Relief mobilizes people through The Power of Bicycles. We are committed to helping people conquer the challenge of distance, achieve independence, and thrive.

Both cut to the chase, unlike McDonald's abysmal effort from a few years back that has all the appeal of room temperature fries:

McDonald's brand mission is to be our customers' favorite place and way to eat and drink. Our worldwide operations are aligned around a global strategy called the Plan to Win, which center on an exceptional customer experience—People, Products, Place, Price, and Promotion.

Uggh. Are they *serious?*

If you are going to have a mission statement:

1. Keep it short and sweet.
2. Limit the population of authors.
3. Determine who it is really for—people inside or outside your organization.

Better yet, here's another option. Rather than spending all the time and energy on a statement that is mostly who you'd *like* to be, why not simply write a statement that captures who you are? Particularly if it is for customers, you don't need the Declaration of Independence or the Magna Carta with grand, lofty statements for the ages. You need a snapshot—not a portrait. Not to mention that few of us have access to wordsmiths who can do an outstanding job crafting the perfect statement.

Here's a snapshot, not a mission statement, of the Community Church, written to give people outside our population a sense of who we are:

The Community Church—A Bit About Us

We follow the way of Jesus
but respect and honor other traditions

We *are* serious about faith
yet don't take ourselves too seriously

We are not bound by historic creeds
but guided by contemporary needs, scripture, and Spirit

We don't say "this is how your faith should look"
instead, we seek to be your partner in spiritual growth

We are an independent congregation
and enjoy the benefits of charting our own course

We don't have members
yet some 350 families call the Community Church "home"

We have no committees or bureaucracy
and encourage all to be engaged in worship, education, mission, and fellowship

We worship in the historic Lily Reid Holt Chapel at Lake Forest College
and believe using existing spaces is good stewardship

We experience nature as a dynamic and inspiring cathedral
holding over 35 worship services each year on the shores of Lake Michigan

We are known for our extraordinary music program
that you need to experience for yourself!

We are committed to experiential outreach
and creatively leverage our resources to support other ministries and charities

We offer inspiring worship, compassionate service, and opportunities for spiritual growth
and somehow, we always manage to have fun…

Garage Sale Buddha

Getting Logo'd

There's an ad running on television right now for a marketing and design company that proclaims, "Did you notice that everywhere you look—from the tops of buildings to the bottom of your shoes—you see logos? That's because they work." I could not agree more—logos are valuable.

The problem is most churches don't seem to understand logos. Upon seeing their logos, my most frequent response is "ouch." Let's just say many don't exactly proclaim "Good News," especially when the logo is a thorny crown resting on a cross. Sorry for the judgement, but unless you're Mel Gibson, a brutal death on the cross is not how most think Jesus wanted to be remembered, or an inviting way to say, "Come on in and join us!" Last time I checked the Bible, it was the meal in the Upper Room on the final night of his life where Jesus told us how he wanted to be remembered.

Church logos often include a cross. On one level I get that. The cross has been *the* symbol of the Christian church for nearly 2000 years. The sad reality is the symbolism and power of the cross has been diminished over the years as the single most overused image in the world—for jewelry, tattoos, design elements on clothing, you-name-it.

And it's not like there aren't any other symbols available for Christians:

- What about the fish used in the early church as a secret symbol to indicate where worship and prayers services were being held for devoted, willing-to-risk-their-lives followers?
- What about the bread of which Jesus said on the final night of his life "when you eat this, remember me"?
- What about a peace sign symbolizing the Prince of Peace?

Yet despite a multitude of options, for some reason churches love to use the cross, which may not be the best idea. Why? No fewer than five thoughts come to mind.

First, a logo should generally not weird people out. The cross—thinking about crucifixion—sends a lot of people's minds in a direction other than God's love.

Second, logos—the visible representation of your church or organization—should differentiate you from peer institutions and competition, not simply mirror what they're doing.

Third, a logo must be memorable if it is going to have any value in the development of a brand.

Fourth, logos should evoke some sort of feeling or emotion that facilitates a connection. When the primary symbol on a logo is the same cross that 75% of other churches have, how is that logo helping you connect with a potential church participant?

Finally, logos should say something—other than you are the same as everyone else—unless your primary branding identity is denominational.

The logo I chose from an online art company for the Community Church now nearly 25 years ago represents the best $125 investment I have ever made. It was my very first online purchase. It is lively, evokes joy, it's colorful and fun and decidedly different from any other church logo that I have ever seen. It reflects who we want to be—people who feel and act like living in God's world is GOOD NEWS!

We've used the logo on everything from bulletins, stationary, and signage, to hats, shirts, jackets—and even trailer hitch covers. We refer to the logo as the "Dancing Bohemians" and it has become such an important symbol that our ten-person Ukulele band decided to call themselves the "Dancing Bohemian Ukulele Team."

Consider your logo, whether you are in a business, church, or community organization. What does it say to you? More importantly, what is it saying to others?

Garage Sale Buddha

Kitchen Cabinet

Traditional church people don't get how I can run a church without having a support structure filled with boards and committees and task forces and teams and volunteers. A better question is "How do ministers who have 'support' structures filled with boards and committees and task forces and teams ever get anything done?"

I believe it's far easier for me to run our church than it is for most of my fellow clerics to run theirs. Why? Because our lack of defined structure means I spend no time jumping through meaningless institutional hoops and playing the bureaucratic games normative in most not-for-profits. Also, what people don't understand is that just because I am not knee-deep in organizational structure and volunteers does not mean that I don't rely heavily on the advice and wisdom of others. The truth is I do—those people just don't have formal positions. They're called the "Kitchen Cabinet."

The concept of the Kitchen Cabinet was first used when Andrew Jackson was elected President. Jackson came into office after a brutal election nearly 200 years ago, and he distrusted everyone in Washington. Seeking to "drain the swamp," Jackson fired long-tenured governmental officials left and right. Then, to make sure he held as much power as possible, Jackson appointed primarily unknown, unproven men to cabinet posts—whom he was confident would rubber stamp his requests.

What Jackson did have going for him behind the scenes was an informal group of trusted advisors who were not officially connected to his administration—but upon whom he relied heavily. They were referred to as the "Kitchen Cabinet".

While the Community Church does not have a Jacksonian cabinet of lightweights who offer rubber stamps, we do have a Kitchen Cabinet of sorts. For example, one person—Kraig Moreland—has been part of that Kitchen Cabinet from a year or two before we held our first service. Kraig is a fellow entrepreneur with a creative mind, a ton of wisdom, and a huge heart. I'd trust him with my life, and except for my wife Jean and my friend and biographer Jay Sharman, Kraig may know me as well as anyone on the planet. How fantastic is it that when I have an issue, a concern, or a golden opportunity I can go to Kraig and trust that I'll get an honest, thoughtful response? Particularly from someone who has institutional memory and understands the players, community, and context.

Would I get that from an elected or appointed board? Maybe, but not likely. Would I get unduly exhausted trying to adjust my leadership style to the wants and needs of new volunteer leaders and board members every few years or so? Unquestionably. Frankly, I do not begin to understand how fellow ministers and priests in traditional churches manage this challenge.

Having a Kitchen Cabinet is not Biblical, though I imagine a case could be made. And, a Kitchen Cabinet is not close to democratic, though I have never pretended that our church claimed this institutional value. The Community Church is not a democracy, and as long as I am around it won't be. It will be run in a manner that is efficient, effective, open, and honest.

With a wonderful Kitchen Cabinet.

On a Dime

A few years back my good friend and international travel expert Michael Stevenson and I put together a trip we called "Adventures in Spirit" for the people of our church. It was a nine-day journey to Nepal, with most of our time scheduled to be spent in the unique, spiritually diverse city of Kathmandu. One week before we embarked on our trip, a devastating earthquake hit Kathmandu and the surrounding area, killing over 1900 people. An additional seventeen climbers on Mt. Everest died in avalanches set off by the quake. Our trip, nearly eighteen months in the making, had to be cancelled.

Yet because we had been tuned into Nepal in preparation for our trip, many felt a need to do something to help our brothers and sisters in the Kathmandu region. A response came to me on the Monday morning following the tragedy while driving to our Lake Bluff office. We'd hold a musical fundraiser the following weekend, just 5 days away, on the street adjacent our office.

I pulled into a parking spot and made call number one to our erstwhile Music Minister Ken Hall, who was scheduled to be on the trip.

"Ken, can you get solid musicians for a Nepal benefit this Saturday?"

"Of course," he replied without hesitation.

Call number two went to Drew Irvin, the Lake Bluff Village Administrator and an all-purpose great guy. "Drew, can we close down the street adjacent the church office and have a block party / fundraiser for Nepal this Saturday?"

"This Saturday?" he replied. "Uh, I don't see why not! Better yet, why don't you hold it on the Village Green and use the Gazebo?" It was a perfect idea that helped make the event significantly better.

Call number three went to the Lake Bluff Brewing Company in our town, to ask if they were interested in selling beer in the park that day for a Nepal Relief Fundraiser. "Sure," came the swift reply from Brewery co-founder Dave Burns. In less than 20 minutes we had the basics in place for the event, from idea to talent to Village approval to beer.

Then I called my buddy (and Kitchen Cabinet dude) Kraig Moreland, who runs the private sports league New Vision Athletics and has a t-shirt operation in his basement. "Kraig, can you help me with setting up a Nepal Relief logo and cranking out a bunch of shirts for this Saturday?"

"Sure, come on over." Not only did Kraig come up with a brilliant design by the time I arrived, but he had the idea of displaying the colorful custom t-shirts we'd have for sale like prayer flags hanging from the trees surrounding the Gazebo.

When Saturday came—and mind you it was the first weekend of May which in the Chicago area could as easily be 40 degrees and sleet as 75 degrees and sunny—we had a warm day and a beautiful, blue sky. It was perfect. The musicians were inspiring, and we even had ten-year-old Nora Sharman stand in the Gazebo and sing a solo for the crowd—all on a moment's notice. Offered her proud fad Jay—another member of the church Kitchen Cabinet—after she sang, "This is the best day of my life. Earlier today at her Little League game Nora had an unassisted triple play. And now this. Unbelievable. It doesn't get any better than this."

And it doesn't get any better than the event, which we pulled together in five days with nothing but word-of-mouth publicity, some volunteer musicians, a raffle, and t-shirts, beer, and food for sale. The Nepal Relief Concert, which was *free*, raised $35,000.

Yes, $35,000.

Support for the event was so broad-based not a single check was for over $2,500. Since then, upon hearing about the fundraiser people have asked, "How did you pull that off in less than a week?"

The number one answer? "No committees." If I had to go to our Board Chair and then our Finance Committee chair and then the Board followed by the Finance Committee and then the Outreach Chair and committee it would have been mid-summer before anything could have happened. By then, it would have been too late. Happily, we don't have all those groups dictating what our ministry is and is not. We do have a group of six people who keep an eye on the money and personnel—but all in a very caring manner. And they trust me to make financial decisions, whether raising money or spending it.

Having no committees and no bureaucracy allows us turn on a dime, make things happen quickly, and take advantage of opportunities. At the risk of spiritualizing it, we can respond to calls from God that would otherwise go unanswered or get lost in a bureaucratic maze.

I thank God for no committees, and how it enables and facilitates our ministry.

Garage Sale Buddha

World's Shortest Sales Class

They say if you want to really learn something, teach it. I realized this was the case when I was a novice windsurfer and rather boldly signed up to take the instructor's course through High Tide Windsurfing in Indianapolis. Of course, there were no tides on Geist Reservoir where we sailed, but that's not the point. Back in the mid 1980's windsurfing was blossoming throughout the world and I LOVED IT! So, I signed up with BIG SSS—the Boardsailing Instructors Group of the Sailboard School System to take their classes and become certified as an instructor. In learning to teach others to windsurf, I became proficient in ways that never would have been possible had I not taken the class. If you want to really learn about something, become equipped to teach it.

The challenge for me as a teacher, though, is that I am by nature a reductionist. I always want to remove what is unnecessary, focus on the basics, and make everything as simple as possible. When teaching beginners to windsurf, for example, about every other word out of my mouth was "balance." The ability to maintain balance—and not become too anxious about falling—is central to being a windsurfer. This focus on fundamentals meant I was a pretty good instructor for beginners, but not nearly as effective for advanced sailors.

This was probably also true when I led sales seminars and programs for corporate training firms. I felt that there were 2 or 3 lessons that were the key to selling success, and that a lot of the material beyond that was just added to make the class longer so the firm could charge more. What were the keys to selling success? Both my own experience and research indicate that the ability to establish trust and uncover customer needs—in large part done by placing oneself in the shoes of the customer—are the keys to selling success. That is, if you understand the world from your customer's vantage point and help them uncover their true needs, you are on your way to selling success.

Put yourself in the shoes of your customers. That's pretty much what I've endeavored to do since starting the Community Church. Since I had lived in the same town with our target population for over ten years, I felt I could place myself in the shoes of at least a reasonable population segment rather easily. They're people who:

- Did not want the politics and bureaucracy that often go hand with churches and religious life.
- Definitely did not want high pressure tactics to either get them to join, provide financial support, or participate in programs.
- Sought messages that fit with today—ones that gave tips or clues on how to live an increasingly complex world.
- Were not interested in feeling guilty, and who were not particularly inspired to get dressed up for church.
- Did not want to waste their time doing inefficient and often meaningless committee work.

We've succeeded at the Community Church in part because we've been effective in placing ourselves in the shoes of our target population.

No matter your job title, most of us ultimately are in some kind of sales. One of the keys to success is placing yourselves in the shoes of those you serve.

Church

*Our home for the last 23 years, the historic
Lily Reid Holt Chapel at Lake Forest College*

Garage Sale Buddha

A Dying Church

One Saturday morning I walked into the small church in the far south suburbs of Chicago where I was to lead a Center for Innovative Ministry "Innovative Church" seminar for six struggling congregations. I was the first to arrive and, finding the front door open, I took a few moments to look around.

Just inside the front door, adjacent the church office, were a series of mail slots. One was for the minister, another for the secretary and the third for the custodian. Underneath were additional mail slots for the church's eight committees. They were the usual committees you'd find in a Presbyterian Church—Building and Grounds, Finance, Christian Education, etc. At the time, I'm quite sure I shook my head, smiled, and thanked my lucky stars that I served a church with no committees.

When the program began in the basement of the church, we took a few moments for introductions. As we finished, I noticed there was no one from the church where we were meeting. I asked the group why there was no one representing our host church.

"Oh," offered one of the ladies from a neighboring church, "they're not here because they're actually holding a congregational vote tomorrow to permanently close the church down. They've had an 85-year-old part-time minister for a number of years and while they have nineteen people on the rolls, they never get more than fourteen people on a Sunday."

I recall thinking to myself, "Isn't that just like a traditional church? They only have fourteen people at worship on Sunday—but they still have eight committees. No wonder they're dying."

It was then that I had a brief "aha" moment. For the first time I realized that churches dying is OK and, in some cases, the very best thing that could happen. A church with fourteen people struggling to stay alive for years is, while admirable on one hand, rather far removed from Gospel messages about abundant life.

Sad though it may be, a church hanging on by a thread is probably more a testament to devotion and habit than faith. That little church in the south suburbs of Chicago needed new life. But before there can be resurrection, death must come.

Politics Free Zone

About 5 years back a huge divide existed between those who were over the moon about our newly elected president and those who were utterly despondent. I struggled a lot with how to address and manage the issue as leader of our spiritually and politically diverse congregation and began to consider the idea of declaring Sunday worship as a "Politics Free Zone."

When I reflected on such a declaration, I envisioned how many of my way-left-of-center seminary classmates and fellow clergy would shake their heads at how I had "sold out" if we as a church bypassed political issues. I heard their retorts in my mind: "If the church is not addressing what is going on in people's lives and the world, whether political or not, then what's the point?"

Additionally, if I said nothing about what were front page headlines in both newspapers and in the hearts and minds of most everyone, it would go against my historic guide for preaching from legendary theologian Karl Barth, who said one should "preach with the Bible in one hand and the newspaper in the other." How would I continue to follow that model of preaching when I was not able to address the dominant news story—Trump becoming president—and the resulting divide?

Ultimately, I decided to declare the church a "Politics Free Zone," and in the weeks following did indeed, receive some curious looks and questioning comments from fellow clergy. Interestingly, I only received one negative comment from a person in our congregation, who in an email stated they were on the fence and "not sure we were doing the right thing by not addressing the issue of our culture's giant divide between pro- and anti-Trump factions." Overwhelmingly, though, the feedback was positive, and we have remained a "Politics Free Zone" ever since.

Why was it the right thing to do? First, because the words I share on Sunday morning are a monologue, not a dialogue. Controversial issues deserve dialogue and debate, and we provided opportunity for that through a series of political open forums we held at the church office where people could speak their peace.

Second, it was the right thing to do because conversation about the new president and the resulting tension for many was omnipresent—people were talking about it everywhere, all the time. Making Sunday worship a "Politics Free Zone" allowed our Sunday service to truly serve as a sanctuary— the one place where people could go for an hour and escape political conversations. Most appreciated it.

Third, it was the right thing to do because the church's role—at least the Community Church's role in people's lives—is not to convince them to see issues a certain way. As in, "You should believe *this* about *that* if you are a child of God!" Instead, we endeavor to partner with people on their individual faith journeys, so they are equipped to make authentic, faithful decisions on their own about challenging issues.

Finally, making the church a "Politics Free Zone" was the right thing to do because decisions should not be driven by what my seminary education dictated, or what's hip these days in other theologically progressive churches. Instead, I relied on our old default question, "What needs do people in the church and community have that we have the capacity to meet?" The answer? What people needed and what we could provide was a much-needed break from the endless political discourse dominating society by offering a space where for at least one hour people could worship in peace.

Following is what I shared with our congregation:

"A Politics Free Zone"

Last night I decided to call an audible and make a change for this morning,

So, I won't be sharing a great teaching of Jesus during "The Way."

Instead, I offer a thought or two about what is happening In the United States of America right now as it relates to the Community Church.

To lay it right out on the table

At the Community Church, we do America—but we don't do politics.

We do America not because God is on America's side But because America is the home

Where we've been blessed with the gift of freedom.

It is a gift we all too often forget or take for granted That allows us to gather and worship in the manner we choose.

And, we owe much to this country and the women and men

who secured and who now maintain that freedom.

But we don't do politics here—either from the pulpit or during joys and concerns.

Partly because the contentious political climate of recent years is more about

Separation and division and judgement and blame Than the peace and justice and service and compassion that are to be

Waypoints during the journey of our lives.

Primarily, though, we don't do politics

because it is not the job of the church to interpret the
secular world
And tell you which side God's on—or which side you
are supposed to be on.
Instead, our job is to equip you with authentic faith and to
be your partner
So you may make wise decisions for yourselves.
This is a sanctuary. A place of peace free from partisan
politics.
This is a sanctuary. Where Christians and people of every
religious flavor—or with no spiritual background
whatsoever—
can peacefully journey together.
Friends, let me close with this:
I can tell you for absolute certain that the Chapel right
now contains people
Who enthusiastically voted for the current president.
And, I can also tell you with certainty that in the Chapel
today are people
Who proudly marched with signs of protest held high
yesterday in the City of Chicago.
And as wide a political gap as exists between some who are
here today
Look at you!
Sitting side by side—singing and laughing and praying
together,
Actively being people of peace and love!

What matters at this Community Church is not that which
divides us
But that which unites us.
And so with genuine enthusiasm
I proclaim the Community Church a "Politics Free Zone"

That we may forever celebrate all that unites us
And the loving Author of Life to whom we belong.

AMEN

Garage Sale Buddha

The Personnel Committee

I don't remember where we were, but I recall quite clearly my feelings when Matt Nagel and Charlie Clarke approached me many years ago after a meeting of our very informal six-person leadership team. "Tom, have you got a minute?" asked Matt.

Charlie followed up, "Yeah, we have something we'd like to talk about if you have time."

"Sure, I'm good," I replied. "What's up?"

They looked at each other as if they already had an idea as to my likely response to their proposal. Speaking in tandem, they told me that they wanted to talk about starting a church personnel committee—though they said since we did not have committees, we did not have to call it that.

I recall responding more boldly than I should have to Matt and Charlie, both whom I really liked and respected— and who had been incredibly supportive of me over the years. "Are you kidding me?" I replied tersely. "That's the last thing we need, or I want. Do you know what a pain in the butt and what a waste of time that is? Is there a problem? Why are you even thinking about this?"

As I spoke portions of my mind were traveling back to a maddening encounter with a personnel committee member from another church years prior. In many ways, things could not have been better at the church I was serving, but I was ridiculously underpaid and after doubling the attendance and the budget I told the committee I felt a significant raise was in order. One committee member privately told me after the meeting that 3% was it and when I expressed my frustration his reply was, "Well, then maybe you came to the wrong church."

So, it's fair to say I had a little bit of "personnel committee" baggage. I finally got ahold of myself and stopped being rude to Matt and Charlie and shutting them down before they had a chance to share their vision.

"Tom," they offered, "we don't want a time-wasting committee any more than you do. Here's what we are thinking. All we want to do is make sure you are all right. Our job is to help you in any way we can. To be your advocates. So, maybe three times a year we get together and have a nice steak and some wine and just see how things are going. How's that sound?"

I don't recall my exact response, but I'm pretty sure I was dumbfounded. Not only was it the exact opposite of past personnel committee experiences I'd had, but it was an incredibly caring gesture on both of their parts. And, in the years that followed, three times a year we'd get together for great meals and wine and conversation and laughter and, a few times, my tears of gratitude. Amidst the demands of ministry, I cannot begin to share how wonderful it was to have a couple of great people say, "We're here for you."

Now that's a personnel committee.

I'm No Different

Throughout history, clergy have been set apart from lay people. They have different titles—they're not Mr. or Ms., but Reverend or Father or Mother or Doctor. Clergy sometimes don special clothing like clerical collars that distinguishes them from the masses (pun intended). Some are prohibited from marriage. Like Jake and Ellwood in the "Blues Brothers," people have seen ministers and priests as "on a mission from God" and thus treat them different from everyone else because of the historic, theological, and cultural sense that they are different.

I'm a bit of a contrarian when it comes to this issue—my position is that *I am not different or set apart* by virtue of my vocation or ordination—which was bestowed upon me by an earthly organizational called a denomination. After all, how is it that a decidedly political organization like a denomination—with most these days struggling for their institutional lives and laden with dysfunctional bureaucracies—has the ability to say, "You are set apart in God's eyes" or "You are not." By virtue of a graduate level academic program? Ordination exams? Demonstrating basic knowledge of Biblical Greek and Hebrew? It's kind of nutty. Ordination often seems far more focused on serving the institutional church than the God to whom we belong.

While I consider it a deep privilege to serve as a minister, I see myself as no different than anyone else. Yes, I have special training and maybe even specific gifts that aid my ministry. However, I believe the primary reason I can be a minister and dare to open my mouth on Sunday mornings is *not because I am set apart, but because I am the same.* I have the same problems (maybe more!) as everyone else in the congregation. And I'm able to preach because I walk the same paths, eat the same food, and experience life in a very similar manner day in and day out as people in the pews.

Last time I checked that's how God chose to communicate with the world 2000 years ago. By sending someone to preach and teach—who was just like us.

Dr. Ward

Dr. John Ward was a local legend in Lake Bluff when I came to town back in 1988. He was an old-fashioned general practitioner who saw patients at his home and kept hand-written medical files on 5 x 7 cards. Many loved Dr. Ward for his devoted patient care and practice of an old-fashioned kind of medicine that no longer exists.

Others were not as enthusiastic about the town doctor, who over the years was able to obtain the two available liquor licenses in Lake Bluff—which he sat on so no liquor-serving bars or restaurants could come to town. Because of Dr. Ward, for years and years Lake Bluff was basically dry, which mirrored the community's roots as a Prohibition-era Methodist Camp meeting town.

Soon after I began serving the Union Church of Lake Bluff, I learned that Dr. Ward was *the* key figure in our church. He was one of the most generous donors, was a consistent and enthusiastic voice in the small choir and was the Church Moderator. It was in this role, which according to the bylaws was intended to be primarily ceremonial, that Dr. Ward wielded significant power. In short, if you wanted to get anything done, you needed Dr. Ward on your side.

A prime example was a few years before I came to the church when a small group led by Elmer Vliet, a highly respected church and community leader, wanted to purchase a pipe organ for the church sanctuary. Dr. Ward was vehemently against it, and so it never happened. The money Vliet and others raised for the pipe organ ended up being used to build a bridge over a local ravine. By the time it was all said and done, in the five years following the fight, the church population plummeted from over 200 members down to 66.

My own challenge with Dr. Ward turned out to be the turning point of my six-and-a-half-year tenure at the church. One day I was in the office about to head out for a racquetball game when Dr. Ward stopped in unannounced. He told me in typical, matter-of-fact style to sit back down, and that it would just take a moment for him to share three thoughts with me.

1. He told me first that I used way too many sports analogies, metaphors, and examples in my Sunday sermons (he was right), and that I needed to cut back on their use.

2. He said we should not read the Apostles Creed or recite it together in church on Sunday because no one really believed it.

3. Finally, Dr. Ward said that reading a prayer of confession and assurance of pardon as part of our Sunday liturgy was inappropriate because the church was not filled with "sinners who committed murders and things like that."

In short, he was not opening a dialogue about these issues, or suggesting that I consider making changes—he was telling me in no uncertain terms what I needed to do.

I had been at the church less about a year, and the key figure in the church, and one of the most important players of the entire community, was telling me what I could and could not do on Sunday morning. Dr. Ward was claiming for himself one of the few powers I had at my disposal to transform the dying church—the shape and content of the Sunday morning service.

As I drove to play the racquetball match, I was furious at the no-win position Dr. Ward placed me. I knew that I had to talk with him—and soon. When my match finished, I spent a few moments with a racing heart at the Lake Forest

Recreation Center parking lot composing in my head what I would say to him. Upon arriving at his home, desperately hoping he was there, I rang the buzzer. When Dr. Ward came to the door, I'm sure he could sense the urgency in my face, and welcomed me in.

I shared with him that he'd put me in an incredibly difficult position. If I didn't do what he told me, it would appear as if I disrespected him and his opinion. If I did what he instructed me, then I would be ceding to him what control I had over my ministry, and basically say "farewell" to my theological integrity—as, at the time, I believed that the Apostles Creed, Prayer of Confession, and Assurance of Pardon were central elements for our Sunday morning worship.

After listening intently to me, Dr. Ward decided to play big-time hardball (see, too many sports analogies and metaphors!). Looking me in the eye with typical seriousness, he said, "Do what you must, but you need to know that if you choose to follow the path you're on I will no longer participate in the Union Church."

My heart was pounding, and my blood pressure surely sky high as I somehow summoned the courage to offer a reply that in retrospect was a little crazy. I matched Dr. Ward's intense gaze, stating, "I would hate to see that happen, because you are a very important person in the life of our church…but if that's what you need to do, I understand. Thank you." With that we shook hands, and I left his office.

As it turns out, Dr. Ward was a man of his word and left the church a few months later. Sadly, he did it in a manner that I believe tarnished his image as one who had done so much good for so many people over the years.

One Sunday, he did not show up for church. It was unusual not to see and hear him singing in the church choir. What none of us knew at the time was that while we were in worship, Dr. Ward was busy spreading one-page letters around the Fireplace Room where everyone gathered for coffee after the service. On the coffee table, bulletin boards and end tables were his resignation as moderator as well as a member of the church. In short, the letter indicated he could no longer support the church with a leader like me.

It was a classic, ugly church conflict, and all I could think was *"holy crap"* as I wondered if I was going to have to leave the congregation and community that in so many ways seemed like a wonderful fit.

Over the next two or three days I spoke with a couple of dozen people from the congregation (OK, about half the church) who admitted they were concerned at what would happen without Dr. Ward, the central figure in the life of the church for the prior fifteen or twenty years. How would we replace his generous pledge? Who would be the new moderator? What would people say?

During those first two or three days there was real concern about the ongoing viability of the church and how we would exist without the rock Dr. Ward had been. Then, on the fourth and fifth days following his resignation a few people began to speak openly to me about life without Dr. Ward.

One admitted that he would love to serve as Moderator, and that "new blood" would be good for the church. A few others told me that while they hated to see Dr. Ward go, it would ultimately be healthy because others could make decisions without first needing to have him on their side. And still others increased their pledges to help cover the shortfall created by Dr. Ward's resignation.

All in all, it was a very difficult situation. I'm sad that in the final years of his life that Dr. Ward made the choice to no longer participate in the life of the church that he had loved. The hard feelings between the two of us unfortunately never went away.

There are three reasons I share the story of Dr. Ward. First, if you're going to run any kind of organization, there will very likely be times when you need to go to the mat (sorry for the final sports analogy, Dr. Ward). Times when you need to risk it all for what you believe in. I refused to bow down and be bullied—at least that's how it felt—by Dr. Ward. I stood my ground, and it was probably the most important move I made in my entire tenure at the church, painful though it was. Sometimes, you need to risk it all for what you believe in.

Second, my leadership approach to just about everything is to always aim for win / win. That's when life is at its best—when everyone wins. To follow that approach, compromise is necessary. For Dr. Ward, there was no compromising, as he was a man who always stood firm and confident in his beliefs. That meant there'd be a winner and a loser. You can't always have win / win.

Finally, successfully running an organization like a church—particularly in a turnaround situation as the Union Church—is not just about creating grand "to do lists" of the tasks you think will make for success. Every bit as important is determining what gets in the way and impedes your success. I didn't know it at the time, but sadly it was Dr. Ward the generous donor, choir member, and long-time Moderator of the church who despite an honest desire to help the church was really impeding its health and growth. From the time he left, the church that had been controlled by Dr. Ward evolved to become a healthy family of faith that's led today by my seminary classmates Rev. Mark and Rev. Tracy Hindman.

Organizational success is not only found in determining what you must do to succeed, but also in uncovering and neutralizing the hurdles and forces that get in the way.

Church Attendance

I found the data in a September 2018 Gallup Poll to be quite fascinating. As most everyone knows, church attendance is trending down.

Church attendance has edged down in recent years. Gallup's latest yearly update from its daily tracking survey shows that in 2017, 38% of adults said they attended religious services weekly or almost every week. When Gallup began asking this question in 2008, that figure was 42%.

—news.gallup.com.

Additional data from Barna indicates a troubling pattern for Christianity in the United States in their "State of the Church" report.

Practicing Christians are now a much smaller segment of the entire population. In 2000, 45 percent of all those sampled qualified as practicing Christians. That share has consistently declined over the last 19 years. Now, just one in four Americans (25%) is a practicing Christian. In essence, the share of practicing Christians has nearly dropped in half since 2000.

—barna.com

The reason for the downward shift? Many offer it's about competition, and all the options that people now have for how to spend their Sunday mornings. Or, in some cases the options people *don't have* on Sunday mornings due to work, parenting, or other responsibilities.

I've speculated that institutional bureaucracies and church values impede change, keeping congregational cultures from effectively adapting to constant social transformation—ultimately making Sunday morning less appealing. Additionally, many churches have an unhealthy inward focus, i.e., "How can *we* grow?" rather than asking "What needs do people in our community have that we can meet?" None of this helps bring people in the door on Sundays.

Senior Gallup Scientist Frank Newport has an interesting take on it that I believe is painfully spot on:

> *A lot of attention has been paid to reasons for the decline in participation in formal religious services. One potential explanation that doesn't receive as much attention as others is the impact of the quality of religious leaders at the church level. Much of our Gallup research for business and industry focuses on the importance of managers for employee engagement—summed up by the statement, "Workers don't quit companies; they quit managers." It's certainly possible that churchgoers don't quit churches, but instead quit ministers, priests, and rabbis.*

Ouch. Newport hits the nail on the head. The institutional church, led in large part by professional clergy——many with a decided touchy-feely nature—would probably never seriously or openly address the quality or lack of strong church leadership today. And most seminaries charged with training church leaders are struggling for their very lives and only partially focused on the needs of the church. I believe Newport is spot on in pointing to something denominational churches will likely never tackle. For a multitude of reasons, the ministry is no longer attracting the kinds of leaders it desperately needs, and it probably hasn't for the last 40 years.

Here's an equally painful question from yours truly that may offer a clue or two as to what's behind the issue:

> *Why would anyone in their right mind choose to enter a profession with high academic expectations, low pay, fewer and fewer churches and available jobs, 24/7 responsibilities, tedious bureaucracies, limited practical training, and a skill set that requires a local church pastor or priest to be an effective speaker, teacher, scholar, fund raiser, manager, and counselor?*

Why would someone want to be a minister? Why would *anyone* want to be a minister? Consider the following data:

- *38% of ministers have seriously considered leaving the ministry in the past year (barna.com)*
- *50% of pastors feel so discouraged that they would leave the ministry if they could but have no other way of making a living (expastors.com).*
- *70% of ministers fight depression (expastors.com).*
- *90% of clergy do not feel trained for what they do each week leading a congregation (expastors.com).*

My guess is there are many reasons people enter the ministry, including the following. One, you become a minister because you feel called. In my case that meant *I simply had to be a minister.* I got to the place where *not being a minister* simply wasn't an option.

Second, people choose to become ministers because they've received significant benefits from the church throughout their lives. They have been loved, cared for, etc., and believe that spending their life in the church will provide an opportunity for those feelings and experiences to continue. They think church life will be awesome!

And it is, until they are expected to grow the church and get people in the door on Sunday morning but haven't been trained in or have the first idea about marketing or communications. Or, they are supposed to create an annual church budget and have never learned a thing about accounting or how to do an excel spread sheet. Or, they get so discouraged from dealing with everyone else's problems 24/7 they become a mess themselves.

There are lots of reasons people do and don't attend church. The very difficult truth in the downward spiral of church attendance is that who leads the church, and how they lead, is probably near the top of the list as to why people do—and do not—attend church. And until denominations and church cultures change and make being a minister a doable job that people are equipped for, it's not going to get any better.

A final thought. One of the reasons I started the Community Church is because doing ministry in a traditional manner was not a fit for who I am. I'm way too twitchy to sit through endless committee and board meetings, and too impatient to deal with bureaucracies. My default is toward action, not process, and I wanted to be able to call my own shots. Having a board or committee assess the merits of every new idea I get and discuss it until we are all blue in the face, or be required to have a worship committee and board approve when we serve communion is to me, a waste of time. If people don't respect me as a leader and trust me to make the calls I need and want to make, having boards and committees to oversee my decisions and behaviors isn't going to make it any better. It's simply going to prolong the dysfunction and pain.

The Community Church has gone from crazy concept to being a healthy and even thriving congregation in less than 25 years because it meets the needs of the people it serves. But as importantly, it is because we've created a culture where being a minister is actually doable.

No Building

Preachers and church types love to say things like "the church is not a building." The truth is, many, many people have a hard time conceiving of a church without a building. In the future, I am convinced that there will be increasing numbers of churches that do not own their worship facility or meeting place.

I embraced the "no building" idea about 25 years ago when I began to develop our church because it made sense economically, environmentally, and practically:

- Why should our attention and resources be focused on maintaining a building when there are perfectly viable spaces available in our community?
- Why should we use precious natural resources and space when we can do fine with what's already available?
- Why should we have all the hassles of owning a building when it's not necessary? After all, we are in the faith business, not the real estate business!

Now, I will admit that not owning a church building / worship center is not easy. Just ask our former Minister of Music Ken Hall or Assistant to the Music Director Daryl Beese, who know all too well about spending Sundays setting up and taking down equipment before and after church. And, while there are number of reasons I drive a Ford F-150 pick-up truck, the top of the list is because *I need to*—I am forever hauling church stuff here and there.

Sometimes, the places where we hold services have not been cleaned from the prior night's event. Picture yourself on the beach at 6:15 a.m. trying to get ready for church and having to pick up half-eaten, sand-covered shrimp and lobster remains, turned over garbage cans that had been invaded by raccoons, and traipsing across a sandy and sticky slab of concrete covered in stale, smelly spilled beer. This is the place that will be our worship home a few hours later. You get the picture. One pays a price for not having a building.

But if given the chance to do it all over, I'd do it the same way again. Because even though it's a hassle, it still makes sense economically, environmentally, and practically.

The biggest problem we face? The world seldom gets people and organizations that go against the grain. A few years back, a person who's active in our church and who previously attended another church was confronted by a leader from their prior congregation. The leader was encouraging the person to return to their family's old church, because they had a new cleric who'd just come to town and whom he was most enthusiastic about. The person in our church politely declined, saying they were happy worshiping at the Community Church, and that their family planned to stay.

The leader's retort? "The Community Church? Why, they don't even have a building! Where are you going to have your funeral?"

Since that story was shared with me, one other people in our congregation had a similar experience. "Where are you going to have your funeral? The Community Church doesn't even have a building!"

This 100% true story leaves me speechless. OK, not really. I just can't write what I'm really thinking...

Competition

Competition is a funny thing. Some people find competing against others uncomfortable, while those with intensely competitive natures are driven to win at everything they do. One very successful businessperson in our church takes it to the next level, insisting, "It's not enough to win— I want to crush the competition."

When it comes to competition, I'm an enigma. As one friend said, "Tom, you don't come across as competitive, but you are *really* competitive. You just choose not to acknowledge it and often pretend like you're not." Touché. Probably true on both accounts.

And churches, I find, are pretty much the same. They are intensely competitive—they just pretend not to be—or pretend to be above that sort of secular behavior. I experienced this firsthand when a fellow clergyperson accused me of trying to recruit people from their church. The false accusations came after our church had a growth spurt that included some dissatisfied, inactive members from their congregation— which was experiencing some conflict. I imagine my fellow minister probably knew deep inside the claims were false and was blaming me as a means of dealing with their own frustrations and unhappiness.

Of course, what struck me as sad is that rather than my fellow cleric looking in the mirror and asking, "What need is the Community Church meeting for these people that we are not?" or "What is it that they are doing that we aren't?" they instead choose to point their finger at me.

Competition in its purest form is healthy and good for everyone. Unfortunately, and particularly in the under-the-radar world of competitive churches, it's far too often Mike Tyson bite-my-competitor's-ear-off-ugly. That's why I believe churches should focus on cooperation, not competition.

First, there are more than enough people to go around, and our focus should be on understanding and responding to people's needs rather than fretting about what other churches are doing.

Second, other churches, perceived by many to be our competition, are generally not our competition. Instead, the competition for churches are youth sports, adult recreation, vacation homes, travel, work, time for rest, and time for relaxation.

Finally, relative to our church, we are so unique compared to the other congregations in our community that it is rare for someone happy at another church to want to come to ours. If they head our way—expecting the more formal style normative in most local churches—they will be disappointed.

The great news is that in our community, churches have moved from a competitive to a cooperative mindset in recent years. We've shared worship services, meals, and enthusiastically supported each other's events. And given that we all belong to the same God, cooperative— not competitive—is how it should be.

KidsUganda

In the early years, the Community Church puzzle was missing a very significant piece. I was always of the belief that churches exist primarily to serve people outside their walls. Our problem as an independent church was finding—in our primarily upper class and already over-served community—a meaningful mission partner. While there are communities to our immediate north with very serious needs, a number of efforts to make connections with them over the years failed. What I knew for sure is that we didn't want to be writing checks to support someone else's program—we needed a mission partner that fit the Community Church's unique and innovative vision of ministry.

My search for that unique mission partner came to an end in 2008 when I attended our local Rotary Club meeting one Wednesday morning. The speaker was the Reverend Patrick Walusimbi, who was in town trying to drum up support for the orphanage and school he and his wife Eva founded in rural Mityana, about two hours outside of Kampala. I listened to Patrick as he told an incredibly compelling story of how he and his wife had started an orphanage and school on a shoestring, and how they desperately needed support for help with orphans and other students who had no access to even the most basic education. Ugandan public school classrooms were often little more than babysitting services, as they often held as many as 70 students in tiny rooms.

As Patrick finished telling the story of the Maranatha School, I sat silently in my chair and had as profound a feeling of call as I'd ever had in my life. I said to club co-founder Fred Jackson, "We have to do something to help."

Following the meeting I approached Patrick to see if he was available to get together. Not only did Patrick have time to meet, but we ended up spending the better part of the next three days together. Before he left to return to Uganda, I told him, "Patrick, I'm coming to visit you. I want to understand more about the Maranatha School and Orphanage, to see what we can do."

Patrick replied with his thick Swahili accent and a characteristically broad smile, "Oh Tom, people say that all the time…but you know, they never come." I believed it was true—as well as a rather savvy challenge. Three months later, I was on a jet making a lonely and frankly rather scary trip by myself to Uganda. I'd never been to Africa and only knew two things about Uganda. First, that the U.S. State Department was recommending against travel to certain parts of Uganda, which is why my friend Tom Pasquesi choose not to make the trip. I'd invited Tom to join me, thinking that traveling with a partner would make the trip more enjoyable and that it would help to have another set of eyes and ears to learn about Maranatha. Second, that the movies I'd seen about Uganda—"Raid on Entebbe" and "The Last King of Scotland"—both scared the hell out of me.

What I found in Uganda after safely making it through the Entebbe Airport (the soldiers patrolling with machine guns thoroughly frightened me) was exactly as Patrick had described. Their need was extreme. He and his wife Eva lived in a single room that would be overly generous to call a studio apartment.

I stayed in Mityana for five days and had experiences like nothing ever before in my life. I met young children at the school with both parents dying of AIDS. Some parents were in the nightmarish position of trying to determine if the

AIDS medication readily available for children—but not adults—should be split between the parent and child to hopefully increase the time before their child was orphaned. I encountered challenges that had never been on my radar screen.

In the years that followed, a simple idea to help the struggling Maranatha School and Orphanage in Uganda blossomed to become a separate charity. We moved it out of the church through the guidance of volunteer leader Wendy Beaver, in part to access additional support that would not likely be given to a church-related program. We also wanted KidsUganda to be an educational opportunity for the children in our community, not just a benefit for children in Uganda.

While never easy—like doing any kind of international business—KidsUganda worked out better than we could have ever imagined during the course of our eleven-year relationship. Africa travel expert Michael Stevenson coordinated over 75 people from our church and community participating on short term "Adventures in Service" mission trips to Maranatha. We provided uniforms, meals, and education. We built dormitories that house orphans and seriously vulnerable children, a kitchen, and other buildings and facilities, in addition to funding a significant expansion to include more than twice as many students. Penny Marsh and Chris Hall led the way by hosting spectacular fund raisers that raised significant support.

Much of this growth came under the devoted leadership of Chair David Andersen, who took KidsUganda to places far beyond what I had ever envisioned. All told, our little church and the KidsUganda charity raised over $1.5 million in support of Maranatha School and Orphanage.

While what we accomplished for Maranatha was hugely important for them, it also impacted our church in very significant ways. There were several years where I am quite sure I spent more time working on KidsUganda than I did our church, and there were a few years when we literally raised more support for the orphanage and school then we did for our own congregation. KidsUganda was one of the best things that happened for our church as people developed meaningful relationships while serving others.

However, over time some began to lose confidence in the direction and leadership at the Maranatha School and Orphanage. While we'd accomplished important work for children at the School, it seemed that their leadership was moving in a direction that did not reflect our values. At the end of 2017, we informed them that 2018 would be our final year of support—which came as a shock to some people who were surprised and sad to see the program finish up after an amazing eleven years.

Most churches have a really difficult time letting their programs and projects come to an end. We feel guilty, and so programs and projects continue on and on and on, even when we don't feel good about it. This is one of the worst thing we could ever do. It saps the energy and erodes trust when maintaining programs and ministries you are no longer enthusiastic about. And, as long as we continued to support the KidsUganda program that many of us no longer had faith in, the longer the period of time that kept us from finding or creating our next transformative mission project.

The best news? While the Community Church no longer actively partners with KidsUganda or the Maranatha School and Orphanage, David Andersen has continued his devoted work that has allowed many individuals in our congregation and beyond to continue directly supporting children at the School.

In the meantime, our church searches for the next opportunity to tackle a need in God's name that we have the unique capacity to meet. Recently, one such opportunity arose when it was clear that many in our community desperately wanted to do something to help people in Ukraine—but they did not know either what to do or how to do it. We decided to leverage two of our strengths, music and organizing community events, and hosted a free, three-hour concert in the local park. Despite temperatures that peaked at 43 degrees that afternoon, the Community Church raised $60,000 for the Ukraine TrustChain, an extraordinary charity that evacuates and aids Ukrainians in the active war zone. (www.ukrainetrustchain.org)

Garage Sale Buddha

Covid Lessons

My friend Toby, a UCC minister in Charlevoix, Michigan, called in the early days of the pandemic. "Hey Tommy, way to go!" he offered in his typically enthusiastic way.

"Tobester, what are you talking about?"

"Man, I've been watching your YouTube services and reading your newsletters and checking out your creative outreach—that Food DRIVE parade you did. Where you drive to get the food? Dude, it's like you are writing a handbook on how churches should be handling this Covid thing."

I was flattered to hear Toby's words, but did not think about them again until another minister friend called and asked for advice on how to arrange for an outdoor worship service during the pandemic. The next day, another cleric emailed me, inquiring about our pandemic services in a local park.

Toby's feedback and the interest of other ministers inspired reflection. I thought about how we'd had 35 new people request to be on our church mailing and newsletter list over the first two months of Covid. And, how we'd kept financial pace despite more than two months of only online services. And, how we had significantly more people watching our worship videos than we could ever fit in our rented Chapel space at Lake Forest College.

What was going on? How is it as a minister—at least during the first few months of the pandemic—I felt more connected to our congregation, despite being disconnected by Covid? The answer is found in two words: simple structure.

When I asked one of the ministers who had called me about our outdoor services if they had anything planned for the outdoors, he shared that they have two re-opening groups studying the possibilities. Another told me he was waiting for approval from the bishop. A third shared their Worship Committee would soon be taking a reopening plan to their church's governing board.

The Community Church had a somewhat different approach. When it seemed like the time was right for us to worship, I called our town's Village Administrator and asked, "Hey Drew, can we meet in the Village Green this Sunday for worship at 10:00 a.m.?"

"I don't see why not, as long as everyone is masked and socially distanced," he replied. I assured him that we would have signs reminding people of this at each entrance, that we'd have extra masks, and make certain the 150 people we thought we'd get would be socially distanced. That was it.

We held the service when the combination of Covid-19 and protests and civic unrest driven by George Floyd's murder were at a peak. We *needed* to be together as a family of faith, as a community—something Covid had robbed us of for the prior 3 months. It felt so good to be together, even if we were socially distanced and not completely sure who that was in the mask next to us.

What facilitated our ability to worship during a time of great personal strife and social angst? It's simple. A nimble structure based on trust. That's it. No other session, vestry, boards, deacons, councils, or committees.

So, how do we get things done with no boards or committees? *It's precisely why we get things done.*

No Middleman

The church is in the business of helping bring God's Kingdom to this world, right? You know—doing the sorts of things that Jesus did and we sense God wants us to do, like feeding the hungry, providing shelter for the homeless, aiding the oppressed, etc. At the Community Church, we say we're about "being the church God calls us to be and the community needs us to be."

At most churches, this part of ministry is usually called social outreach or mission, which is the sum of all the good works a church does for those who exist outside their walls. In some cases, social outreach goes well beyond direct human needs to include environmental and other kinds of global issues. These works are often partially paid for through fundraisers and special events like rummage sales, but outreach is typically a line item in annual church budgets. For some churches it's a few percentage points, while other churches "tithe" with 10% or more going to outreach / mission.

At the Community Church, none of our annual budget goes for outreach.

WHAT? You selfish dogs!

I know, when people hear that they are sometimes befuddled, and ask, "What's up with that?" It's a legitimate question. Why do we not give money to outreach? The answer is: "We do—just not in traditional ways." There are several reasons why.

When starting the Community Church, one of my goals was to neutralize issues that made participating in a church a challenging or negative experience. One of the areas that often causes strife is outreach giving—or where church mission dollars are sent. For example, during stewardship season in every Presbyterian Church I have ever served the name Angela Davis comes up. Angela Davis was a Black woman activist and Marxist / communist who owned weapons used in a California courtroom takeover where 4 people died. She was jailed for over a year while awaiting trial, but ultimately acquitted on all charges. The Presbyterian Church—then called the United Presbyterian Church in the United States of America (UPCUSA)—gave the Angela Davis Defense Fund $10,000, ostensibly to help ensure a fair trial.

And what do you think happened back in 1970 when word got out to local churches that the national Presbyterian Church gave a Black, Marxist / communist woman $10,000? You're right! Countless Sunday coffee hours were abuzz with heated conversations and untold individuals and congregations considering withdrawing some or all of their support from the national church. And, while some applauded the bold move of the UPCUSA Council on Church and Race's grant to the Davis Defense Fund, on a purely practical level the decision had a devastating impact for decades.

What's amazing is that while the decision is no longer the raging fire it was in the 1970s and 80s, embers from fifty years ago still burn for some individuals and congregations. People still talk about Angela Davis today, and I'm certain that there are a few who support their local church—but instruct their church treasurer not to allow any of their donation to support the national church.

The most significant fallout from the UPCUSA / Davis controversy, however, was the erosion of trust in the decision making of the church. Once trust wanes, it's really challenging to recapture—and it's impacted the Presbyterian Church for decades.

While the merits of giving to the Davis Defense Fund can be argued back and forth all day long, the truth remains that it's very easy to make a well-intentioned decision that turns out to be unwise or perceived as such when directing other people's money toward social causes. A common refrain these days at many churches is "Why are we supporting people on the other side of the world when we have so many problems here in our own backyard?" While I'd argue that a balanced approach to outreach is best and that we need to reach out both near and far, I get what people are saying. The bottom line? It's just not worth getting into an argument over, which is what churches do all the time.

But far and away the biggest reasons we don't include outreach as part of our annual budget has nothing to do with avoiding conflict. In the first part of the twenty first century, it makes no sense for a church to serve as a middleman for individuals in their charitable giving. One hundred years ago, the church played a key role in our world distributing financial and other resources to people seeking assistance. If you wanted to helping starving people in India, you gave money to the church that knew how and where to put it to good use. This was a need the church was able to meet. While imperfect, the church was able to be experts in outreach and mission.

Today, if you want to help others, you can go online and find all the information you need on how to donate, how your gift will be used, the percentage of donations that are used for administration, and more. These days, technology has supplanted the church as a middleman. If you have $10,000 available to help others, are you going to go online and do a little research on how your donation can best be put to use, or are you going to hand it over to a church committee that may or may not put it to use in a manner that reflects your values and wishes? In 2022, people don't need the church as a charitable middleman.

Yet another reason we don't support other charitable organizations—beyond our desire to neutralize potential conflicts and avoid the inherent inefficiencies of mission committees—is that we've discovered that our Situational Approach to Mission (SAM), at least in the context of the Community Church, yields far greater results from multiple angles than a traditional model.

SAM is based on the following very simple principles. First, people can participate or not—it is their call whether to be involved and to what extent. Second, SAM is hands on. We don't just write checks like most mission committees. Third, SAM is typically funded by events, which yield significant fellowship and community relations benefits.

Over the years we've hosted multiple SAM events, some of which have been highlighted in this book, like the Ukraine Benefit Concert. Another classic example of our situational approach to mission were the KidsUganda Benefits. Held in a stately area home, the catered events with music, entertainment, raffles, and more raised hundreds of thousands of dollars to support the Maranatha School and Orphanage in Mityana, Uganda. No church budget dollars were expended, so people who believe only in local mission did not have the chance to get upset. We had great fun creating and hosting the events. It provided those outside the church with an easy entry point to step into our church culture.

The list of benefits we received from KidsUganda SAM events is almost endless, though the ultimate beneficiaries were the children in the rural Ugandan village who were fed, clothed, educated, and cared for in ways that would not have occurred without our support. In the end, it was a lot more meaningful than taking a portion of the church budget and then having a committee argue over whom they should write a check to.

Garage Sale Buddha

Public & Private Courses

*"... I'm just a soul whose intentions are good
Oh Lord, please don't let me be misunderstood."*
—the Animals

Once upon a time there was a town with six golf courses. Five of the courses were private and catered only to their members. The sixth course was public and open to anyone who wanted to play. The 18-hole track was started by an affable, journeyman PGA professional who was a surprisingly marginal player himself. It seemed he could help others with their games—but struggled with his own game. What made the public course unique is that it had an expansive practice facility, and no restrictions on its use—it was available to anyone all the time, no questions asked, from sun-up to sundown.

Over the years the historic private courses with manicured fairways, lightning-fast greens, and abundant amenities thrived, while the public course struggled to stay afloat. In fact, few people in the town even knew the public course existed, and if they did, they paid little attention.

That is, until one day when a foursome from a private course could not book a tee time at their private club and headed to give the public course a try. The foursome was, in a word, surprised. "What a refreshing change of pace," offered one.

"Yes, I really like the open layout," said another.

"No fancy clubhouse, but I like their style. They do a good job here," replied a third member of the foursome, "I'll be back."

Soon the public course began to see more and more people plying its fairways and greens and using its unique practice facility. At the same time, some of the private courses noticed a reduction in rounds played and a number of players dropping their memberships—including a few who had begun to play at the public course.

Rather than ask their players why they left the private courses, or ask themselves, "What need does the public course meet that we do not?" the PGA pros pointed their fingers at the public course pro and accused him of stealing their players. One said he purposely hired an assistant pro who had ties from 25 years ago to the private course to lure members to the public course. Another filed a complaint with the state PGA accreditation committee and the United States Golf Association, claiming the public course pro was operating outside the bounds of what was good for golf.

The public course pro vigorously fought the accusations, all of which were shown to be unfounded. Yet the damage had been done, and for several seasons relationships between most of the private courses and the public course were frosty, particularly as the public course grew in popularity.

Things changed when the public course pro met with one of the private course pros, a friendly guy named Mike, who seemed to respect what the public course was trying to do. Mind you, the two pros and their respective courses were different as night and day, but they shared a common passion for the game.

One day at a lunch meeting, the two decided they'd work together to try to change the relationships between the pros and the courses for the better. It began with all the pros gathering to have lunch meetings at each other's courses. And it continued when two engaging and highly skilled professionals named Luke and Clint came to town as head pros at a couple of the most prominent private courses, and the public pro reached out to welcome them.

"Let's get along," was the message the public course pro shared. "There are plenty of golfers in this town for all of us. And in the end, it is not about our courses—it's about the game."

In the years that followed the whole feeling about golf in the community changed. Joint tournaments were held. Courses promoted each other's events. Golfers enjoyed trying new courses without upsetting previously possessive pros. It felt good, especially to that old public course pro, who'd always felt that the game does not belong to the players, but that the players belong to the game.

Garage Sale Buddha

For Members Only

A woman in our church who'd attended for a year or two came up to me after worship one Sunday and asked, "Hey Tom, how come we don't have members?"

I'd reflected long and hard on that question over the years, but unfortunately, I gave her a smart-ass answer. "Because no one has ever given me a good reason why we *should* have members." Understandably befuddled, I took it one step further for her. "I don't mean that rudely; I just honestly can't think of a reason we should ask people to sign on some sort of dotted line. And I can't remember anyone saying, 'You know, I wish we had a membership program.'"

Curious why we don't have members? Other than because "I can't think of a reason we should," here are a few additional reasons:

- Denominational churches must maintain membership rolls to pay per person head taxes which we do not pay.
- We can tell how we are trending as a church without the metrics that often misleading and easily manipulated membership data provides.
- We prefer to measure our impact by the work we do in the community rather than numeric growth measured by membership gains.
- Not having members or a spiritual required standard—i.e., "You have to affirm that you believe what we believe in order to join."—keeps the door wide open for people who simply seek to inquire.
- Members make more sense for clubs, where the role of member implies both institutional responsibility and a form of ownership; neither is

119

the case at the Community Church where participants have little or no institutional responsibility or ownership—we exist only to the extent we are effective in meeting peoples needs.

- Membership organizations typically allow their members to vote on matters from annual budgets to choosing leaders; neither is the case at the Community Church—the votes people make at our church are through (a) attendance and (b) financial support.

A final, very important thought on membership. When you join most churches, you sign a statement affirming that your beliefs are in sync with those of the church you are joining. Where does that leave the person who is uncertain of their beliefs? Or the inquirer who's never been part of a church and has no idea what they believe? Or the person who likes the church and supports everything they are about—but disagrees with a portion of the statement of beliefs? They have little choice but to sign their names with hypocritical hesitation or not become a member.

This does not seem right. After all, isn't the primary issue not where you are spiritually when you join us as much as where you'd like to go? To start the church membership journey with an affirmation of firm and confident beliefs seems like welcoming someone to the finish line before they run the race.

Wouldn't asking people to craft a vision statement for their spiritual future—not a membership document on what they believe then and there—be most appropriate?

A final thought. Doesn't "belonging" to a church emphasize the wrong thing? Shouldn't the emphasis be on our belonging to God

Kool-Aid

A recurring, hopefully not belabored theme in *Garage Sale Buddha* is all that differentiates the Community Church from other churches:

- We don't own a church building in which to hold services.
- We don't have members.
- We are 100% independent.
- We don't have committees or a bureaucracy, except for a six-person board that exists to keep an eye on finances and personnel.
- We use existing spaces in the community such as the beach, parks, the local college, and the local community center for worship and programs, which both supports their work and allows us to use resources for ministry, and not for maintaining buildings.
- We have no choir, and music style ranges greatly from week to week.

Yet for all that differentiates us from other churches, one thing stands out head and shoulders above the rest—*we don't make you drink our Kool-Aid.*

OK, it's a bit crass, but it helps make the point that we, unlike every other church I know, do not require that people say "yes" to a single model of faith if they seek to be part of the Community Church.

For example, if you want to join the Episcopal Church, you are asked to embrace the Anglican model. If you seek to become a Catholic, you're required to say "yes" to the Roman model. If you are going to be a Presbyterian, it's the Reformed model. You get it. In every other church I am aware of, they all say, in far more polite language, "You have to drink our Kool-Aid. You have to say 'yes' to our faith model if you want to join and become a member." In short, it is a fundamental job of individual churches to perpetuate their historic model.

While imperfect, this method of institutional propagation has worked. Roman Catholics have kept it going for nearly 20 centuries. Reformed churches for 500 years. Not bad! What business or organization would not be delighted with a multi-century run!

The problem is there are clear indicators that the church is no longer working either as it has or as it should. The Roman Catholic Church is too large to function effectively, as the needs and values of followers from Central America to Europe to North America to South America to Asia vary greatly. For example, traditional Catholicism found in Italy is radically different than the liberation theology that informs much of Roman Catholicism in South and Central America. It's more than one organization can effectively manage.

Protestant churches are struggling mightily, as well, as the Presbyterian Church (PCUSA) where I was baptized, confirmed, and ordained has lost more than a million active members during last 14 years (2005-2019). As of 2020, the PCUSA has 1,245,354 active members. Equally startling is that not that long ago—1986—the denomination had over 3,000,000 members (pcusa.org)

Religious organizations of every flavor are struggling and, in some cases, dying. In the United States, in 2020, 47% of Americans said they belonged to a church, synagogue, or mosque, down from 70% in 1999 (Gallup). Membership in American religious organizations are down by a third in just 20 years! Clearly something's not working.

How does the Community Church exist in such a "down market" when nothing is trending well for organized religion? We focus on the needs of individuals, believing the job of the church is to be a dynamic spiritual partner and a source of inspiration—not to preserve an individual brand or model.

Garage Sale Buddha

Innovation

Garage Sale Buddha

Experts & the Micro Church

I was fortunate to participate in the McCormick Seminary Doctor of Ministry program. By a wide margin, it was the best educational experience of my life, equipping me with tools to help turn around the Union Church as well as start the Community Church. I'll be forever in debt it to the people—from generous donors to enthusiastic professors to dedicated administrators—who made McCormick happen back in the 80's and early 90's. However, I can't say there wasn't a hiccup or occasional frustration in my D.Min. experience. Consider my monstrous thesis disappointment.

As I approached the end of my program, having finished seven of the nine required classes, I needed to gain approval for my thesis. I knew exactly what I wanted to write my thesis on—the Micro Church—which was the label I chose for the vision of what I dreamed would someday become the Community Church. If I had listened to the "experts," though, it never would have happened.

Like micro-breweries that produce smaller batches of high-quality beer, the Micro Church would offer a minimalist, focused ministry. We would not provide programs that clergy spend absurd amounts of time and energy on to persuade peoples' participation. Instead, the Micro Church would focus on two things:
-   Providing high-quality, inspiring worship each week.
-   Meaningful pastoral care.

And, we might have a party every now and then. But being a Micro Church meant there would be no Sunday school, no youth ministry, no bureaucracy or committees, no outreach, no Women's Guild, and no weekly Bible Study. The Micro Church would be a new model of the church that was all about feeding and caring for people—not about building a "successful" church in the traditional meaning of the word—which was lots of people and lots of programs.

I spent quite a bit of time creating a thesis proposal for the late Dr. Carl Dudley, a highly respected McCormick professor, author, and consultant. I needed Carl's OK to move forward. After I handed him my proposal, I sat across from his desk watching him read through the giant Harry Caray glasses perched on the tip of his nose. Anxiously I waited, noticing every time he'd smile or squint as he read. When Carl finished, he cut to the chase. "OK. Well, it's pretty interesting, Tom. But I don't think this works as a thesis."

I was dumbfounded, as I anticipated both approval and praise for my outside-the-box idea. "Carl, what's the problem? I don't understand."

"Tom," he replied with characteristic compassion, "your Micro Church is intriguing. The problem is it will never work."

"Huh? Really? Why do you say that?" I started to push the respected church guru, maybe in ways I should not have. I was ticked.

"The biggest issue," Carl replied, "is the Micro Church doesn't have connection points. Your Micro Church has no way for people to become engaged or connected to the church culture. There are no groups, no committees, no programs where people can get involved. I just don't see how it will ever work."

To say I was disappointed is putting it mildly. I was downright dejected, and ultimately wrote my thesis on image and identity formation for small, not-for-profit organizations. In the end, it was a valuable project that aided me at the Union Church, Lake Forest College, the Community Church, and with many clients I've advised.

I took Carl's advice to heart, and for almost ten years I set my vision of the Micro Church aside, having lost confidence that it would work. Over time however, I simply could not let go of the Micro Church—an idea that I truly believed could work. When I finally committed to creating the Community Church around 1998, part of me was fueled by the expert who told me what I could not do.

While I don't regret not starting the Community Church sooner, I sometimes wish that I had—if only because given the extra time I might have been able to have had a far greater impact and take it *deeper*. Who knows?

Carl was a great guy, and a skilled researcher. But I think he knew mostly about how the church *had* functioned—and not how it would need to function in a rapidly changing future.

When starting something new, it's undoubtedly wise to consult experts. However, be careful about letting experts overrule your heart—which in my experience is where we most often hear the voice of the Spirit.

Garage Sale Buddha

Bears vs. Packers

It's been said, "There's no such thing as a bad idea." Creativity guru Derek Sherman offered a variation on that theme when he said, "There's no such thing as a wacky idea." I get that. However, there are plenty of ideas which if implemented will do more harm than good. Consider the following two stories.

When I started our church, we did not have the money to buy shiny brass offering plates—though I probably wouldn't have bought them if we did have the money. So, each week we *literally* "passed the hats," which usually were whatever baseball hats I grabbed from around the house before I headed to the service. Hats were also nice because they provided a soft landing for the welcome but sometimes embarrassing-sounding coins.

Well, a of couple days before a big Monday Night Football Chicago Bears vs. Green Bay Packers game, I got an idea. Instead of using my old baseball hats for the offering, why not pass football helmets! We'd have one for the Bears on the left side of the church and the other for Green Bay on the right side. What an idea!

Well, it certainly was "cute," and I got lots of pleasant comments on how creative I was. But based on the significant lack of money in the two helmets, it seemed there were plenty of Bear fans who said, "I'm not putting any money in the Green Bay helmet" and vice versa. They identified their giving with supporting or not supporting a football team—not the church.

It's an example of a well-intentioned, creative idea that in the end did more harm than good. My error? It's one I've made plenty of times. I didn't take the time to think through the possible results of my creative "genius," or consider the impact of possible scenarios. In retrospect, the idea was good—it just needed different implementation.

I did do a variation of the idea a few months later with Santa Hats during the Christmas season instead of helmets during football season, and then on Easter with old-fashioned Easter bonnets. They worked great as both Bears fans and Packer fans love Santa hats and Easter Bonnets!

Many years after the Bears and Packers helmet service, I was speaking to a group and a person far wiser than me heard the story—and made it much better. He asked, "Why not pass both helmets to everyone—and they get to choose which team they want to support? And then you have someone count the proceeds at the end of the service and you can announce 'which team won.'"

It was a great idea and would have made a good idea much, much better. Don't be content with a cool idea! Take the time to make it great.

Windblessed Weddings

Most ministers are interested in hearing the story of The Community Church. They're intrigued by our no building, no member, no committee philosophy and how it works in practice. Most also love to hear about our summer Worship on the Beach services, and how we've continued to grow during a time when so many churches in the United States are struggling After hearing our story, it's not unusual for someone to dream out loud about someday starting their own church, too.

But if they stick around long enough to hear about the price they must pay—they begin to understand that it's a crazy idea—and near impossible to start a church from scratch while taking no seed money from outsiders.

Frankly, in looking in the rearview mirror at all that has transpired over the last 20+ years the whole thing was probably nothing short of insane. Jean's work was at home raising three young children and we barely had enough income to support our family, let alone subsidize a Church. I'm still not sure how it all worked out beyond a combination of remortgaging our house, using what little savings we had, taking very few vacations, and not having much in the way of stuff, at least compared to others in our high socio-economic class community.

Starting a church ourselves was a crazy idea, and I did everything under the sun to make ends meet in a way that allowed me to still have time to begin the church. Among my jobs were serving as Special Assistant to the President and Director of Marketing and Communications at Lake Forest College, working as the Vice President of Business Development for Vacala Construction (Jesus may have been a carpenter, but I had absolutely no business in the construction business), starting a company called the Dickelman Idea Group which offered corporate training and a variety of consulting programs, and becoming a landlord by renting our house. How I did all these things while starting a church and keeping our family together, I'll never understand. I'll be forever in debt it to my wife Jean for her support in allowing me to do what she knew I simply had to do.

One of the great challenges I faced in the early years of the Community Church was starting a business called "Windblessed Weddings." Basically, I was a minister for hire available to officiate at Chicago area weddings. In creating the business, I put together a website, advertised in local wedding magazines, and made sales calls on local hotels and bridal consultants who might need an officiant.

I probably reached one of my lowest points when I found myself one Sunday morning at a Chicago area resort for their annual bridal fair. That's right—this minister was not at church, but at a bridal fair. There I was in my little booth—with a florist on one side and a wedding DJ on the other—trying to promote myself as a wedding officiant. It was nuts.

In between schmoozing brides, and usually their mothers, I could not help but ask, "What the hell happened to me?"

- I'd jumped through seemingly endless hoops in a four-year oxymoron-ish "Care Process" to become ordained, in addition to three years of intensive seminary / graduate school.
- I'd had spectacular internships, including basically running the Chicago Lawn Presbyterian Church myself for a year and working at the storied Fourth

Presbyterian Church on Michigan Avenue in Chicago.

- I received the chance of a lifetime to work with Bill Enright at Second Presbyterian Church in Indianapolis, which under his tenure became one of the great churches of the Presbyterian (PCUSA) denomination.

- After a year-long sailing sabbatical I was able to help turn around the dying Union Church of Lake Bluff where, in six and a half years, I had an exhausting but wonderful experience.

- I'd also received a Doctor of Ministry degree from McCormick Theological Seminary.

Somehow, I had gone from positions of respect, and in some cases real success, to being at what most would consider the absolute bottom of the pastoral barrel—working as a "rent-a-rev" minister doing weddings at local hotels, meeting halls, homes, rental chapels, beaches, you name it. And while the DJ in the booth next to me was a really good guy that I actually ended up working with a few times, it was one of the most humbling experiences of my life.

The bottom line? I'd do it again. Being a "rent-a-rev" was basically what I had to do to help fulfill a vision I believe God blessed me with. It was a way to make an extra $15,000 a year, and at that stage of the game when I had little income and was subsidizing the church with our savings, it made the difference between keeping our family afloat and sinking into a sea of debt. And, while driving around the Chicago area most Saturdays rushing from wedding to wedding—I once officiated at four weddings in a single day—was not exactly a great way to spend time, the truth is I met many, many wonderful couples. I made the conscious choice not to care what others thought about my descent from prestigious pulpits to minister-for-hire, and in the process discovered that I loved the privilege of officiating at weddings.

People always like to say that you can do anything you put your mind to, and I believe that to be true. The greater question is, "Are you willing to do those things that are really difficult, and that most people will never understand?"

The Dancing Bohemian Ukulele Team

I am a musician wannabe. Which is to say, I like the idea of playing music and singing on stage, I just don't want to (a) learn to read music, or (b) practice. I'll practice occasionally, but only enough so I can play the dozen chords or so I know on the guitar or ukulele.

Many years ago, likely inspired by the scores of exceptional musicians that Ken Hall brought into our church each Sunday, I announced to my wife Jean that I needed to *seriously* take up an instrument. I'd been a mediocre guitar player since college, and I needed to learn to play something.

I considered numerous instruments, including the accordion. How hard could it be to move a squeeze box back and forth while playing a simple keyboard and pressing an occasional button? Well, I found out rather quickly that it would be plenty difficult. Mostly, though, I knew inside I'd never have the discipline to stick with it. The accordion was a "nay."

Then I officiated at the wedding of McCamie Cole, the son of our beloved former church Administrator "Tiny Ted" Cole, and his bride Kate, who now works with young children in our church on Sunday mornings. Following the ceremony, a wonderful reception was held in a converted barn where there was no shortage of food, drink, dancing, and celebration.

The highlight, though, was when the band stopped playing and McCamie pulled out a ukulele and played and sang the classic "You Belong to Me." If you don't know the song, you might remember it from "The Jerk" starring Steve Martin and Bernadette Peters. In the movie, Martin sings the song to Peters while playing the uke. Then to everyone's surprise, Peters grabs a trumpet and belts out a few lines with Al Hirt-like energy. Which is exactly what Kate did—surprise everyone by playing—*well*—her bandleader grandfather's trumpet. It was a great moment in my wedding Hall of Fame.

After being wonderfully moved, I told my wife Jean that I was going to take up the ukulele. The next week I did just that and bought my first uke. Immediately, I was a bit bummed because the soprano uke required that I learn an entire new set of chords different from a guitar. Knowing how my brain works, I was not sure that was going to happen (I ended up with a baritone uke so I didn't have to learn new chords). Then things changed when I asked one friend, then two, then three friends—all serious, skilled musicians who played guitar—if they wanted to start a ukulele band with me. To my surprise, they all immediately said "yes" and in less than a week our new band had our first practice.

When our Music Minister Ken Hall got wind of what we were doing he said "Hey, I want to be in that!"

"Ken, you play vibes, piano, percussion, recorder, and who knows what else. But I've never seen you with a string instrument in your hands," I replied.

"So what?" Ken said. "I'll learn." Which is exactly what he did, and soon we had five then six then seven and now ten members of what I named "The Dancing Bohemian Ukulele Team" after the church logo which we call the Dancing Bohemians.

We practiced every Monday afternoon—a bunch of musicians and a minister. Our first "gig" was on the Fourth Sunday of Advent when we played a variety of Christmas tunes in matching red and black Santa Hawaiian shirts. Much to the amazement of the congregation, we sounded pretty good!

Then something really interesting happened. People started to ask, "Where can I get a uke?" and "Where can I learn to play?" Of course, I saw this as a gimme when it comes to opportunities, so I bought 8 ukuleles that people could rent, asked master guitar player Elliott Delman to serve as teacher and director, and the Community Church's "Dancing Bohemian School of Uke" was born.

In recent years, our band has performed at church services, weddings, picnics, and other special events. Much to my amazement, some folks are even willing to pay us to play! Today, we have eight musicians (and me!) in the band, including our newest member Bob Hasty, who is an Associate Professor of Orchestras at the Northwestern University Bienen School of Music. Every time we play, these great musicians and me, I feel like a 20-handicap golfer who gets to play in a foursome with touring PGA pros.

The point of all this? After nearly 40 years of ministry, I believe all the opportunities you'll ever need will come to you. The key is to live with an open heart and an open mind. The Dancing Bohemian Ukulele Team is just one example. Other musicians were looking for an outlet to have fun and play music together. Then people were so pumped to hear us play—sensing the fun we had—they wanted in on it. So, we started a School which further connected people with the church, in some cases provided a valued parent-child joint activity, and gave our musical director additional income. Finally, people in the Community heard about us via word of mouth, this "church with the Ukulele Band and School," enhancing our profile among our targeted, outside-the-box population.

None of it was particularly difficult and none of it was planned. The entire ukulele program evolved organically, and it began by paying attention to what's going on in people's heads and hearts.

Aquatic Experience

The thick paper stock gave the church bulletin a formal feel—appropriate for the cathedral-like sanctuary of the traditional 2600-member Second Presbyterian Church of Indianapolis. The font was formal as well, and likely chosen more for style than readability. On the back page, the list of ministries was extensive—reflecting a dynamic program with abundant resources, including seven ordained clergy on staff. Nestled among the programs like "Open Forum," "Adult Bible Study," and multiple choirs for all ages was a ministry I led for people in their twenties and thirties and offered twice per week, entitled "Aquatic Experience." Any guesses what "Aquatic Experience" was all about? Was it:

- A program addressing the spiritual / religious use water, such as its role in the sacrament of baptism?
- Classes about the miraculous stories of water in the Bible, from Moses parting the Red Sea, to Jesus turning water into wine, to his walking on water?
- Something else?

Where does "Aquatic Experience" lead you?

Frankly, it was a tongue-in-cheek name chosen for a program I started, sufficiently classy to be acceptable yet clearly absurd for the largest land-locked city in the United States. Aquatic Experience was a ministry where I taught young adults to windsurf at Geist Reservoir, which evolved to become one of most enjoyable and successful ministries in which I've ever participated.

Windsurfing became a passion of mine early in the 1980s, and I became certified as an instructor. I volunteered to teach the classes at the Hi Tide Windsurfing Shop and School (not sure about that name as there were no tides in Indy) for free if they'd reduce the price for the classes I taught to people from the church. It was a win on multiple levels, and unbelievably fun, and I loved doing ministry on the water in God's glorious creation. It provided great exercise and developed both community & new relationships…and got me out of the church offices!

Most of all, though, windsurfing—and you know this if you've tried—provided a level playing field for everyone. It didn't matter if you were smart, athletic, overweight, popular, needy, successful, nerdy, Christian, whatever. When learning to windsurf, everyone loses control, everyone falls off, and everyone gets soaked and looks a little silly before humbly pulling themselves back on the board. All the preconceived notions about who someone is or is not, the kinds of things that often impede the development of healthy groups, start to vanish when everyone—*I mean everyone*—loses control and "gets baptized" in the water.

Now, did we talk about Jesus when learning to windsurf at Aquatic Experience? No. We got wet, laughed, sailed, and often had a beer after class. Did we build community, deep friendships, and open the door to meaningful ministry down the road? Without a doubt.

And it began with a simple, innovative idea of joining two worlds seldom mentioned together in the same breath— ministry and windsurfing. That's partly what entrepreneurial and innovative thinking is about—bringing divergent elements together in creative ways to meet a goal. Author Robert D. Hisrich defines an entrepreneur as "an individual who takes initiative to bundle resources in innovative ways and is willing to bear the risk and/or uncertainty to act." (*Entrepreneurship*, 8th edition, McGraw Hill Irwin, 2010).

How does one begin to think entrepreneurially and bring diverse concepts and ideas together in a manner that benefits your ministry, organization, or business? Without getting into a deep debate (not unlike that of speaking in tongues—is it learned, or from "elsewhere"?), I believe many elements of entrepreneurial thinking can be learned.

And the starting point for learning to think innovatively, and with an entrepreneurial spirit begins by answering these questions:

- What do you love?
- What's your passion?
- What are you willing to go the extra mile for?
- What do you know inside and out?

Typically, what we are passionate about is what we know best. We understand the idiosyncrasies and the details. We notice and begin to understand patterns. For example, when I was learning to windsurf, I learned that *everyone crashes* when they start out. Soon, you begin to make natural connections with other areas of your life. I realized that everyone crashing while learning to windsurf was ideal for developing group dynamics—not to mention spiritual commonalities. It's a small but important step toward thinking in a new and creative way.

If you seek to develop innovative solutions and programs in your work, and do not see yourself as one of those "creative types" for whom it comes naturally, spend some time reflecting upon:

- What are my life passions?
- What do I know about those passions? What elements and patterns are present?
- Do any elements or patterns fit with the core issues of my work?

In the Aquatic Experience example, I was passionate about windsurfing. I saw the consistent pattern of everyone, *everyone,* who learns to windsurf losing balance and falling awkwardly into the water. That experience created a common bond among participants—a dynamic that's present in healthy groups and communities.

Over the years I've been involved in creating innovative ventures that range from Aquatic Experience and Walk on Water contests to an Organic Garden to founding the Dancing Bohemian Ukulele Team. At the most basic level, it's about bringing divergent or unique elements together in a manner that typically provides multiple wins.

Worship on the Beach

I started our ministry over 23 years ago. Initially, it was called "The Community Worship Hour." We met each Saturday afternoon at 5:00 p.m. for worship in a local college Chapel and took the summers off. For three years, the Community Worship Hour did OK, but there was a very unhealthy pattern.

The pattern was that from September through May of each year we'd gradually grow and develop momentum, only to lose it all during our summer hiatus. The result was that each fall, it felt as if we were starting all over again. The answer to the problem seemed obvious—we needed to hold summer worship services. *Where* to hold services became the real problem:

- Our ministry did not own a building in which to hold services.
- We did not have access to the College Chapel during the summer.
- We had no money, *none*, to rent space for summer services.

In short, we were up a crick without a paddle. What could we possibly do, and where could we go?

The answer came one day when I was at the beach in our town, which is located on the shores of Lake Michigan. The beach is a place where I go to unwind, and sometimes pray. If you are not familiar with Lake Michigan, it gives you the feeling of being on the ocean—just without saltwater or sharks. From where our town is located, it is about 75 miles straight across to Michigan. As I walked barefoot in the soft sand looking for beach glass the answer came to me—*Why not meet on the beach?*

The more I dreamed about it, the more ideal it seemed.

- Everyone knew where the beach was located.
- There was an open-air shelter in case of inclement weather.
- Early on Sunday mornings the beach was quiet, except for the occasional kayaker or sailor, which added to the ambience.
- The beach was beautiful, and, maybe best of all, as a public space *it was free!*

On the Sunday after Memorial Day, 2002, we held our first service on the beach. I was psyched to "preach on the beach!" Of course, as often happens with "outside the box" entrepreneurial efforts, it took a while to catch on. That's my way of saying there were three people at our first beach service—Becky and Steve Freeman-Murray— and me. Never held a worship service at a picnic table before! Not exactly a world-class start, and it made me move a little toward becoming a Biblical literalist as I remembered Matthew 18:20 "where two or three gather…" We sat at the picnic table, talked, prayed, and I shared a few thoughts in the only sermon I've ever delivered to just two people. Needless to say, it was easy to maintain eye contact with the congregation…and hard for them to doze off.

Now, many years later, "Worship on the Beach" has become one of the innovative elements for which the Community Church is known. We are the only congregation I know of on the North Shore of Chicago that has more people show up for services during the summer.

- Services on the beach begin a week before Memorial Day and continue through the end of September.
- The summer prior to the pandemic we averaged 225 people each week at our two Sunday services.
- There's live music each Sunday including special "Blues on the Beach" services.

-   We offer baptism in Lake Michigan and unique events like our annual Children's "Walk on Water" contests and a "Closest to the Pin" competition using the beach as a giant sand trap.

And, we've continually tried to understand what attendees wanted and needed in order to maximize the experience for them. We purchased tents to keep people who could not find a seat in the shelter a way to be stay out of the sun, and bought beach toys for kids. Transportation was added up and down the hill before and after each service to make it easier for some to attend, and Kate Waltman lobbied the Lake Bluff Park District until they purchased 40 yards of heavy rubber mat that allows people with disabilities and in wheelchairs to attend.

What may be best of all about Worship on the Beach is that it provides an incredibly easy way for people to invite their friends to church. We know "friends inviting friends" is the number one reason people initially come to our church. When someone asks a friend or neighbor "Want to come to church with us this week?" and are able to add, "And by the way, church is at the beach," it makes coming to church pretty difficult to pass up!

The lesson in all this? I have no idea if holding services on the beach ultimately was the result of my innovative thinking, dumb luck, or the Holy Spirit. The truth is, I don't know and don't need to know. What I am certain of is that innovative solutions are sometimes the result of little more than refusing to give up.

The Retreat

I probably heard the questions at least a half dozen times at the retreat after people glared at my nametag. "Tom Dickelman, why, I remember *that* name!"

- "Where have you been?"
- "Whatever happened to you?"
- "Are you still in the ministry?"

Good questions, I suppose. You see, I was with a group of Presbyterian ministers on a retreat. We're affiliated professionally but we have very limited interaction during the course of a year, and after being invited for twenty years to attend their annual retreat, this was the first one I'd made.

In response to their questions, I shared what turned out to be for most a universally baffling story—about how I could start a non-denominational church within a quarter mile of a prominent Presbyterian denominational church— and not be *defrocked* by the denomination.

Moving beyond their befuddlement with my unique situation, I was peppered with questions. Some which sounded, frankly, as if they were coming from denominationally incarcerated clergy—curious about life outside the institutional church from one who had successfully escaped.

I shared the story as a few leaned forward in their chairs—eyes opened wide. I'll admit a not-so-healthy part of my personality took over that delighted in telling the story. Kind of like playing it up when you tell someone about your refreshing, ice cold glass of lemonade—and you know they are dying of thirst.

"Yup, I rented the Lake Forest College Chapel, sent out some postcards and that started it," I offered.

"But what's the church like?"

"Well," I replied, "we have a couple of hundred active families—but don't have members. There's one board of six people for the entire church, and they meet for breakfast three times a year. We have no traditional church building. We rent an historic Chapel with Tiffany windows on the Lake Forest College campus during the school year. And every summer service is on the beach of Lake Michigan."

"No boards, no elders, no deacons, no trustees?" they asked in amazement.

"Nope."

For some, I think it sounded too good to be true, and I understand that. After all, in denominational circles, size matters. Good, bad, or indifferent, it's a primary means by which institutions measure their churches and clergy. To hear of a church where there's no annual discussion of net gains or losses must have sounded pretty appealing.

And, for clergy who have committees up the...shall we say, *"up the ladder all the way to heaven,"* having a single board that meets three times per year for breakfast—that's it— probably sounds quite appealing, too. The same goes with those who have buildings requiring ungodly amounts of time and capital resources, as well as those who get tired of the same old, same old and secretly yearn to do something like preach barefoot on the beach.

After a few questions and answers, a fellow clergyperson seemed to want to poke holes in and deflate the story of our church. "Yeah," he probed, "but do you do any outreach, or anything for those outside your own church? I mean, if you're not in a denomination how do you do mission work?"

I responded, again probably with too much pride, "You know, that might be the best part...over the past 5 years, if you include the charity in Uganda our church started, dollar-for-dollar we've probably raised more money for people outside our church than we have for ourselves." That pretty much ended the questions about our church.

I've reflected quite a bit on that retreat in the time since it occurred. A couple of things strike me. First, I think I was all too happy to tell the story of our church because I am not regularly connected to other ministers, and deep down inside I wanted to gain the respect of my fellow clergy. If we were in a denominational church and went from an idea to 350 families in roughly 20 years, particularly with no debt, rainy day money in the bank, and having started a charity which we ultimately funded to the tune of $1.5 million—I'd be a star that church officials would point to and say, "It can be done! Look at that!" It's tough to admit, let alone put on paper, but I was *really needy and wanting affirmation* from my peers. I'm passionate about innovation and our independent church, but there's a downside to innovation and independence. Both can be lonely, and innovators are often misunderstood. I have felt both.

Second, taking the pastoral road less traveled is like most other journeys—people are interested in the end destination, not what it took to get there. My fellow ministers were curious about our church, but no one really asked, "What did you do to get there?" I did not hear:

- "What did it take to develop your congregation?"
- "How did you finance the church?"

No one cared that I started the church with my savings and a second mortgage on our home (not recommended) and then served the church for three years without pay. Or, that to help make family ends meet I started "Windblessed Weddings"—the business that helped me connect with people who needed a wedding officiant. Trust me, you'll meet every "spiritual but not religious" person on the planet if you get into the weddings-for-hire business.

Want to be humbled? Envision seeing your name alongside a dozen other wedding officiants in *Chicago Wedding Today* magazine who got their credentials online in ten minutes for $25—while knowing you spent seven years and tens of thousands of dollars earning a master's in divinity and a doctorate in ministry.

Excited to be an innovator? Have an entrepreneurial spirit as do I? Wonderful! Innovative thinking can provide many of the answers our on-life-support churches need. Just remember that if you choose an alterative path, you'll pay a price for being different, just like you will pay a different kind of price if you travel the worn roads of the majority.

In the end, it's all about determining how to get where you want to go.

Creativity

It is safe to say that this will be the only vignette that begins with a reference to pornography. It's because when trying to define "creativity," what initially occurred to me is that it's similar to what Supreme Court Justice Potter Stewart said about pornography. Stewart chose not to try and define it, but offered, "I know it when I see it."

We know creativity when we see it, right? It's a new way of doing things. It's unfamiliar yet pleasing takes on familiar concepts and forms. It's the unexpected that flows from an unconstrained soul. We could probably reflect and comment on the various layers and definitions of creativity until the sun goes down and comes up again. That's not our goal. Instead, I want to consider the role of creativity as it relates to ministry. Two distinctly different quotes on creativity help us move in that direction. The first:

"Creativity is using old things in new places, ways, and combinations."
—Professor Robert Sutton, Ph.D, Stanford University

Bill Hybels is the founder of the Willow Creek Church in Barrington, Illinois that became a leader in mega-church, evangelical Christianity. Whether you love Hybels or think his ministry symbolized all that's wrong with religion in America these days, what remains true is that Bill Hybels is a creative genius. Some say it's about marketing, not creativity. Whatever. The bottom line is that he took something old—traditional worship—and presented it in a new way. Hybels took the sizeable challenge clergy deal with every week, preaching to both believers and non-believers, and came up with a simple, amazing solution: Have two services. *Duh!* Why didn't I think of that? One service for seekers, the other for believers. Brilliant! Bill Hybels created a new way of doing church by making a few relatively simple adjustments to what already existed.

The second quote on creativity:

"Creativity is the quality that you bring to the activity you are doing. It is an attitude, an inner approach—how you look at things."
—OSHO, Indian mystic and guru

During our summer Worship on the Beach services, we hang scores of Tibetan prayer flags each week from the roof of the open-air shelter. Some flags have lost their color over the years and are slowly wearing away as if having fluttered for years at a frozen Mt. Everest base camp. Others maintain their bright, out-of-the-box primary colors. About a third of the flags have been made by families in our church, with colors and symbols reflecting their family's prayers for the summer. The prayer flags add a spiritual feel to our space and provide me the annual opportunity to share their meaning and the belief that as the flags slowly weather and disintegrate, the symbols on the flags go out as prayers into the universe. The flags are a joy, and I receive comments each year on what they add to our worship experience.

If I'd seen them as (a) exclusive to another tradition, (b) unchristian, or (c) entirely inappropriate, we'd not enjoy what they bring to our services, including the chance to reflect on what it means to pray.

Creativity is a bit like God—in the end, something of a mystery. And just as prophets throughout history have pointed us in the direction of the divine, Sutton points us toward understanding creativity when we consider using what currently exists in new ways. OSHO is also helpful when he encourages our seeing the creative enterprise as how we view life.

Over the years, the Community Church has frequently been commended for its creative approach to ministry. Like growth that comes as a result of doing the right things for the right reasons, I think our creativity is the result of thinking like Sutton and OSHO. It's not so much about fashioning something new, as it is seeing what exists in new ways.

Change = Opportunity

Put yourself in the chair I found myself in today. You're seated at the conference table mid-morning in the upstairs office. Surrounded by windows on three sides, all you can see is snow. It's coming down *big time*. They've closed the schools and library, programs have been cancelled, and kids have taken over local restaurants, sledding hills, and whatever gyms they find open. What does that mean for you?

Opportunity.

Why? Because anytime things change there is opportunity. It does not really matter what changes. Just know that whenever there is change, there is opportunity. For example, what would you do with these "change = opportunity" scenarios?

- A church member demolishes a dilapidated home they own in your community. Their plan, because of the changing marketplace, is to plant grass and sit on the property as an investment. Where's your opportunity? (We planted a garden on the lot and gave the produce to a local pantry).

- A local landlord is seeking to rent the space she owns in her downtown storefront. Traditionally, people have covered the windows with paper whenever a retail space is available, with only a small "For Rent" sign in the corner. Where's your opportunity? (Two artists in our church created a three-dimensional image of our church in the window accompanied by a paragraph of creative copy about our ministry).

My guess is that if you took five uninterrupted minutes to reflect on the snow day, demolished home, or storefront scenarios, you could come up with multiple opportunities for your ministry. What would you do?

This morning in a snow day note that took all of 5 minutes to write I sent a message to our church family. The email postcard read as follows:

THE COMMUNITY CHURCH CAN HELP!

If you need help because of the big snow—whether it is a ride to an appointment or assistance clearing your drive—please call our office at 847 234 8191. We have volunteers ready to help anyone who's in a pinch.

– TD

Within thirty minutes I had over fifteen responses. Ten people responded with comments like "Thank you!" and "I am so glad to be part of a caring church!" and "I am OK, but it is good to know you are there!" The other five people wrote replies like "My snowblower is ready and so am I," and "I've got a big boy truck—let me know if anyone needs help." I had more than thirty responses—all affirmative. In twelve hours, I received only two requests for assistance, both easily taken care of.

It was an investment of ten minutes to let people know they were cared for, and that we have people lined up if they needed help. It sent a message that they can count on their family of faith when they are in a pinch. And it happened because of recognizing that most every kind of change = opportunity.

Falling Short

An amazing squirrel, Lutz, Florida 2021

Garage Sale Buddha

A Smorgasbord of Tidbits

I'm wired to be a sprinter. Not an athletic, Usain Bolt kind of sprinter, but a sprinter who is always rushing from here to there and from this to that. It's how I live most days, speeding around as it was my last day on earth. In most everything I do, I want to get there quickly, to maximize time so I can do more. For example, I actively think through the fastest way to travel from Point "A" to Point "B"—which route has the fewest stoplights, whether there is right turn on red, etc. I want to get things done ASAP. Sometimes, it means I am successful in cramming ten pounds of life into a five-pound bag (so to speak). But it can also mean, amidst my zeal to be swift and move onto what's next quickly, that quality of experience and "being in the moment" get tossed out the window.

As you might guess, sprinting through my classes was not necessarily the best way to approach college and seminary. I got away with it at the University of Utah in the mid to late 1970's, which was a wonderful place to ski and, oh yes, get a degree. When it came time for seminary, a rigorous three- or four-year graduate school program, I learned the hard way that zipping through the syllabus to get 90% of the work done in the first two or three weeks of the semester was not the way to go. In "Greek Exegesis of the Gospel of John" I *really* learned my lesson.

Basically, without knowing any Biblical Greek (which was central to the class), I attempted to write my mid-term paper—about a third of our grade—the first two weeks of class. Why not? Get it over with and then move onto other, more enjoyable and interesting things, right? That was the idea, at least. I wrote the paper and was happily on cruise control for a few weeks before turning the paper in the day it was due.

Less than 48 hours later—way ahead of schedule—the paper was returned to my seminary mailbox in a discreet, brown envelope. The brown envelope turned out to be an academic body bag, intended to shield the public from a paper that had been deemed dead on arrival by the professor.

In opening the envelope, it looked like Professor Anne Wire's pen had exploded on the ten-page paper. I'm not sure I took a breath as I read her remarks, so aghast was I at the *assertive feedback* she provided.

On the final page Prof. Wire summed up her feelings about the paper, and me, I think. "**TOM**," she wrote in bold large letters, **"THIS PAPER IS A SMORGASBORD OF TIDBITS AND I CAN'T FIND THE MEAL! SEE ME IMMEDIATELY!"**

Ouch. She was so right. That paper was a disaster, and I felt like such an idiot. My sprinter personality was more interested in swiftly jumping through a hoop than getting an education, and then rushing to what was next on my agenda. For me, I was trying to fit the seminary into how I was wired and wanted to live, rather than adapting myself to be in sync with their traditional educational model.

Upon reflection, I suppose that's in part why I designed the Community Church as I did. The traditional church in many ways had not been a fit for me. And, while I created our church based primarily on my perception of community needs, I also wanted a church that suited how I was wired and sought to live my life. To survive and do what I truly felt called to do, I needed to create a church that fit me. And now a few decades later, I am so glad that I did.

"Church" With a Small "c"

One of the problems with churches is they often think it's about them. About their members, their buildings, their programs, their mission strategies, etc. It's not a good place to be, because the church that was started in the first place to serve God and spread the message that Jesus brought to the world often ends up taking precedence over the God they are called to serve.

Certainly, this issue is present in churches of every flavor, and has been a particularly difficult issue in the Roman Catholic church in America, where some very powerful Bishops made the choice to not report blatantly illegal acts perpetrated by priests. They did so, I assume at least in part, amidst their zeal to serve and protect the church. However, in the process they lost sight of what the church is supposed to be in the first place. They serve a church with a capital "C"—which is what occurs when the priority is the church rather than the teachings and values of the one upon whom the church was founded.

I understand how this can happen. I was once told by an underage student who was part of an international exchange program that he had been targeted and sexually abused by an adult in our community. My first response beyond caring for the victim was decidedly unchristian—I wanted to rip the perpetrators' throat out with my bare hands. My second thought—after I had settled down—was "What if this goes public, and the program which has benefitted thousands and thousands of students around the world is destroyed because of what happened?" It broke my heart to think that an extraordinary international program that did such good could come to an end.

Just then I thought to myself, "Oh my gosh. This is how it happens. I'm worried about this amazing program dying—rather than justice for the abused and consequences for the abuser." I'm embarrassed to admit this ever came to my mind, but it did. This is the sort of thinking that has kept abusive clergy in the ministry. People more interested in protecting the church than perpetuating the values the church was formed to proclaim.

Fortunately, I realized the seriousness of the accusations and immediately contacted a friend—a local judge—who shepherded me through the process. The good news is that now many years later the student is wonderful—happily married and a proud parent. The judicial system did its job, and the perpetrator was appropriately punished. We need to trust the systems our society has in place to administer justice, difficult though it may be at times.

As for the church? The church is about the journey. It is about helping people develop and maintain a connection with God, and about bringing God's kingdom to this world. Unfortunately for many, church has become a destination unto itself.

"Church" should be spelled with a small "c."

"Even If You Win the Rat Race…

…you're still a rat."

That was my motto for a time back in the days when I started the church. Part of my idea in starting a Micro Church was to avoid the pastoral version of the rat race, where many nights are spent in meetings and 24/7 work is the norm. I loved the idea of starting an independent congregation, but it needed to be one where I could actually have a life outside of the church. And, as importantly, I wanted to model the kind of life that I did not see much of in our community—one with balance.

Now, more than twenty years in, I can say without hesitation that my vision of leading a healthy, balanced lifestyle while starting and running a church has been an utter failure.

Maybe the "success" of the Community Church makes it seem like I won the rat race. In the process, however, I've become a big-time rat. Rather than lead my brothers and sisters to the promise land of healthy living, I've gone the exact opposite direction and become a workaholic. How do I define that? The church and her people are pretty much what I think and talk about way too much of the time. Deep down inside, I think I like having my truck parked outside the church office at all hours and have people say "Wow, Tom, you're always there." It's kind of sick.

What's crazy—and what should serve as fair warning to all—is that in the early years of my ministry, if I were arrested for being a workaholic I'd *never* be convicted. My case would be laughed out of court.

While I worked hard at my job as a young minister, I always made plenty of time for golf and handball and beers and vacations and friends and windsurfing and all the extra stuff in life that I enjoyed. For example, to make certain I would not miss out on a sweet day of sailing, on Sunday morning I used to park my old Saab 900S in the six-car minister's parking lot at Second Presbyterian Church in Indianapolis with my windsurfer on the roof, ready to go immediately following the last "amen." More than once, I was asked why no one saw me at Coffee Hour following worship. My answer? "Hello! Check the trees! The wind was blowing 12 to 15 mph! I couldn't miss that!" I had swiftly traded my robe for a wetsuit and was windsurfing with mostly don't-go-to-church pals at the local reservoir while Second Church folks downed another Styrofoam cup of Folgers.

Then in my early 40's as I started the Community Church—with the expressed goal of living a healthy, balanced life benefitting the community and me—just the opposite occurred. I became consumed by the ministry. Maybe it was because serving others in God's name was incredibly fulfilling. Maybe meaningful work became more enjoyable than recreation. Maybe it was because I had a family of five to support and a mortgage to pay and failure was not an option. Maybe all of the above.

Now, in the autumn of my ministry, I've at long last started to ease away from the workaholism that defined the last 25 years. In part, it's because I don't have the Energizer Bunny get-up-and-go I used to. More than that, though, is that the entire church no longer rests on my shoulders. Today, I am blessed with trusted co-workers led by my fellow minister Sean Miller, and I regularly experience the benefits of a team-based ministry.

The great benefit of the Micro Church design that became the Community Church was that I had control, and in broad terms success or failure was in my hands. The great drawback of the Micro Church design was that I was in control, and for most of our history I was actively involved in every element of our ministry. It forced a workaholism that I had neither the strength nor the discipline to effectively manage.

Were I to do it all over again, what advice would my 60's self give my early 40's self? "Develop and maintain a consistent prayer life." For there is little question that a clear correlation exists between the quality of my prayer life and being the person God wants me to be, and that I want to be, as well.

Garage Sale Buddha

A Sermon / Confession

When Barat College closed, buildings were both repurposed and demolished. Developer Bob Shaw—a kind and generous man— called to see if our church had interest in saving the old but not particularly historic or memorable Chapel. While it seemed to be a long shot, I figured I had nothing to lose so I drove over to meet Bob and tour the space.

I recall three things about the Chapel that day. First, it was very dark inside, so unless we put in a retractable roof like they have over Miller Park in Milwaukee, it would never work for our church. Second, the pews were so uncomfortable that it would be impossible for people to fall asleep in them—which of course for a preacher like me was a plus! Finally, off to the side of the Chapel was a small, dusty confessional booth crafted of depressingly dark wood. It was eerily silent and as lifeless as anything could be. I idled next to the confessional for a moment imagining the human stories and the raw pain shared in that space during decades of countless confessions.

Frankly, as a non-Catholic, confessional booths kind of give me the willies. However, I also find them to be quite intriguing. Maybe it's the intensity, or at least the potentially intense experience that comes with being able to openly share what is tearing you up inside. Or, the feeling of being unshackled from the wages of sin because of the grace extended to sinners by a loving God.

The most intriguing confessional booth I'm aware of is the one best-selling author Donald Miller writes about in *Blue Like Jazz*. Miller and friends set up a confessional booth with friends at Ren Fayre, a weekend of absurd, over-the-top partying at Reed College in Portland, Oregon. Miller and pals in the College Christian group built a small shelter—kind of like a storage shed you might erect in your backyard—and placed it in the middle of the music and dancing and drunkenness and debauchery and drugs that is Ren Fayre. It seemed akin to placing a block of ice on a bonfire—way out of place and certain not to last.

However, that's not the whole story. Miller and friends did not set up the booth to *take* confessions; they were not there to listen to their classmates' tales of how they cheated on tests or stole their roommate's beer and blamed it on someone else, or lied to parents about their grades. Instead, Miller and his Christian friends built the confessional booth for "reverse" confessions—to confess to their non-Christian classmates all the ways that Christians and the Christian church throughout history had sinned, fallen short, and not come anywhere close to mirroring the love and grace of Christ.

Suffice it to say they blew plenty of people out of the water as they admitted to carrying their own agendas in conversations about Jesus, and mixing spirituality and politics.

So today, on this Fourth of July weekend, we're not going to turn this space into a confessional booth where one by one you march up the steps with me on the other side of a cloth and ask you to offer confessions, whether it is the weight of sin making your life unbearable, or as a child who has to make something up, like, "I didn't eat all my beans." No, we are not going to go that route. This Gazebo is just a little too public and "Sound of Music-ish" for a confessional booth.

Instead, in the spirit of Donald Miller and his friends from Ren Fayre at Reed College, today I apologize and offer a long-overdue confession to all hearing or reading these words. About things that anyone whose been paying any attention at all already knows. Namely, that Christians throughout their 2000-year history, and the church that is supposed to be the earthly home of God, have fallen desperately short of the goal of loving God and loving neighbor time and time again. We have been woefully inept at doing God's work.

Sadly, "falling short" as a phrase to describe our behaviors falls short itself. You see the church and we Christians at times have not just been clueless but have actively—aggressively—acted in ways that must leave our Creator sobbing in absolute disbelief and disappointment.

And so, as an ordained minister and part of the church universal, but nonetheless a self-appointed representative, I apologize to you and confess that I and we have made a mess of God's work from start. My hope is that you will recognize all this mess is a reflection on us, and not the God to whom we belong.

Friends,

- I confess that the Crusades—nearly two centuries of bloody battles and death all ultimately over a piece of land—were an exercise in insanity with complete disregard for the lessons taught by the one known as the Prince of Peace.
- I confess that the genocide Columbus committed in the Bahamas was—horrifically—in God's name.
- I confess that emboldened missionaries who felt they had a corner on the truth disrupted and destroyed the lives and cultures of Indigenous People throughout the world.

- I confess that the church throughout history has all too often stood by and condoned slavery and racism, and tolerated oppression and injustice.
- I confess that the church has frequently judged those who looked or sounded or loved or acted differently than we are, and we have excluded them from the Kingdom audaciously believing that it was within our power to do so.
- I confess that the church has not challenged princes and powerful who used position to promote themselves and keep down others, and that we have not healed the broken, cared for the sick, clothed the naked or fed the hungry while our own cupboards were full and our lives abundant.
- I confess that the church and its clerics have abused power and people and all too often swept it under the rug—foolishly tricking themselves into believing it was the right thing to do.
- I confess that the Community Church has taken pride in our uniqueness, watered down the radical call of discipleship, focused too intently on our own needs and too little on those of God's Kingdom, and put trust in our work ethic—rather than our trust in God.
- And, as leader of the Community Church, I confess to being self-centered and inconsistent as a spiritual guide and co-worker, and regularly acting like I pray more than I do, and appearing more faithful than I probably am. I am a hypocrite, and have failed God, my family, and you. For all I have control over, and for all I do not, I humbly seek your forgiveness, and God's grace.

The bottom line? Writer Sean Claiborne said it well, "I am sorry that so often the biggest obstacle to God... has been Christians." I think he's right.

Friends, if your excuse for not pursuing the spiritual life has been bad religion, clueless churches, corrupt clergy, and hypocritical adherents, it is entirely understandable. We have missed the mark of accurately reflecting the light of God's love into the dark places in our world. But at the risk of being rude—*get over it.*

Please don't let the sins of the church or the hypocrisy of ministers and followers get in the way of directly experiencing God on your own. Neither you nor I need a middleman or intermediary. Amen.

Garage Sale Buddha

Words

Just prior to my final year of seminary, I wrote a letter to the legendary minister Elam Davies of the Fourth Presbyterian Church of Chicago looking for a part-time job. In the letter, I pointed out my experience in the ministry (which I now realize was ridiculously limited) and how Fourth Presbyterian would benefit from giving me a job. It was more than a little ballsy, and quite a longshot, as I'd heard they'd not hired seminarians for over two decades. I figured I had nothing to lose, though, and amazingly, I was hired and blessed with an incredibly memorable and valuable experience.

Dr. Davies was from Wales, maybe 5' 6" tall, and at the end of a storied career in the ministry. He'd made his mark in the pulpit, and in 1979 was named one of America's "Seven Star Preachers" by *Time* magazine. Just before he retired and I graduated from seminary, I scheduled a meeting—ostensibly to glean whatever wisdom I could from the renowned preacher.

Stepping into his office, Dr, Davies offered me a seat on the couch just inside the door. It was a "lowrider" couch—like you might have when you are broke in college—where you sink awkwardly close to the ground. Davies, meanwhile, sat across a coffee table from me in a large, upholstered chair that positioned him higher than even his tallest guests. I'd found out during my time at Fourth this was an "Elam thing." In whatever room he was, whether attending a meeting or enjoying a Christmas party, he always scouted out the chair that would hoist him as high as possible.

After no small talk—I think he was wondering (for good reason) why he agreed to meet with me at all—I asked him my best question. "Dr. Davies, after all your years in the ministry, what's the most important advice you can give to someone like me, who's just starting out?" He replied swiftly, as if it were a question he'd been asked multiple times. His response was both clear and impassioned.

"Words," he replied, with the Welsh lilt he used to his advantage so beautifully in the pulpit. "Be careful with your words. You can spend your entire ministry doing good work building the kingdom. And all that. Then with a few, poorly chosen words it can all come tumbling down. Just like that. Be wise in choosing your words…"

I am not sure what I expected to hear, but it wasn't that. The man who was a legendary wordsmith, who made his life with words and became famous with his words was warning me of their danger. Like gas that powers an engine, words are flammable and could blow everything up if not treated with care. Just ask golfer Phil Mickelson, whose poorly chosen words have cost him an estimated $40 million in annual sponsorships and put a cloud over his Hall of Fame career.

It's now been four decades since I sat with Dr. Davies. Upon reflection, I regret not having done a better job implementing his sage advice. Often in a desire to be funny, I have hurt people with my words. I've frequently been less-than thoughtful with my words. I've used words as weapons at times, and often talked more like a truckdriver than a man who is allegedly trying to bring God's Kingdom to this world.

As the saying goes, "be careful with your words. Once they are said, they can only be forgiven, not forgotten." Clearly, words to live by.

Sucking at Golf

An important existential question I've pondered is "why do I suck at golf?" Upon reflection, I think about 20% of my issue is the result of physical challenges due to an aging, marginally cooperative body and a lifetime collecting sports injuries. Five dislocations, three surgeries, bone spurs and arthritis in my left shoulder alone doesn't help my swing. Another 20% has to do with my knowledge of the game, which is OK but not what it could be. The remaining 60% of my struggle with golf is almost certainly *between my ears*.

That's right. As any of my golfing buddies will tell you, I am something of a head case when it comes to golf. I have a very limited capacity to focus, and frequently after finishing a swing I realize that rather than concentrating on the shot, my mind has wandered off into la-la land, lazily reflecting on topics as varied as how I'd fare on *Hot Wings*, electric trucks, or how hoodies have become fashionable on the PGA Tour. My lack of focus is a bit maddening, and it's not unusual that after a few double bogeys (or worse) by the 6th or 7th hole I stop keeping score.

One issue with sucking at golf and only breaking 100 half the rounds I play comes when I have a new playing partner, or when I compete in matches as I did a half dozen times last summer. After a few holes that very likely include my dribbling a tee shot sideways 30 yards into the bushes— or even a complete whiff—I begin to sense my playing partner and opponents appearing baffled and a little embarrassed. It's really awkward. The look on their faces asks, "How could someone who seems reasonably intelligent and kind of a regular guy—especially for a minister—be so bad?"

It's kind of like making a new acquaintance who seems great but when you visit their home, everywhere you look is a mess—and it doesn't make sense that a likeable, seemingly normal person could live in such a disaster area. My game is the disaster area, and after playing partners witness it for the first time, I spend the remainder of the round trying to show that while I may be inept as a golfer, I'm not really as bad of a person as I am a golfer. And yes, if you are saying to yourself, "This guy doesn't need golf lessons, he needs therapy," I understand.

The other problem with sucking at golf is that all my regular playing partners have much lower handicaps, which means they're significantly better at golf than me. To make our matches fair they give me strokes. So, if I take 6 shots on a hole and they take 5, I still win on many holes even though they played better. While handicaps are designed to even things out between players of varying skill levels, it's a lose/lose proposition for someone like me. Victory is hollow when you get strokes to even out a match, and if you win too often then you're a "sandbagger" and accused of having too high of a handicap and getting more strokes than you deserve. The bottom line? You can't win as long as you suck.

So, why do I continue to play, when the odds at this stage of the game of my becoming a decent golfer are pretty slim? Because in golf, no matter how I play, I still win. For many like me, the score is a small part of the game. Golf is about cherished time with friends and family. Fresh air. Laughter. Challenge. Exercise. And nature, which I actually get to see quite a bit of based on the interesting places my golf balls land.

As I prepare for the upcoming golf season, my hope is to accept that "my gifts are in areas other than golf" and to have gratitude for the consistent joy golf brings to me, no matter my score. As Mick Jagger of the Rolling Stones croons, "You can't always get what you want, but if you try sometimes, you just might find, you get what you need."

I seldom get what I want on the golf course, but I almost always get what I need.

Garage Sale Buddha

This I Believe

I don't recall the either the time or exact place of our conversation, though it was when I was preparing to leave Second Presbyterian Church of Indianapolis after 3.5 years of peaks and valleys service as an Assistant Minister. What I recall from the conversation is how I felt afterwards—sick to my stomach.

I was with Bill Enright, my boss at Second and spiritual father now for some 50 years. I asked him a very pointed question that I almost immediately realized was both insulting and hurtful. While I don't think about it often, when I do, I still feel bad.

On that fateful day, evidently having checked my brains at the door, I asked Bill, "You know, I have listened to you preach as a member of your church for many years, and now for over 3 years as part of your staff. We've spent a lot of time together over the years. But through it all, I'm not completely sure what it is you believe."

Frankly, it hurts me to recount the story, because Bill is one of the best people I have ever known. He is a great human being who *lives* his faith. The kind of person I envision God pointing to and saying to all the rest of us "Hello, pay attention to this Enright guy, would you? He gets it."

I honestly don't remember how Bill responded to my question. But over time I've come to understand that Bill was not the issue, but much more likely my inability to either pay attention or effectively grasp his deep and thoughtful messages.

Fast forward nearly four decades to the Community Church studio and office at the Gorton Community Center in Lake Forest. Sean Miller, our Co-Minister who has been an absolute gift to our church family and to me, had just read a draft of this book. I asked Sean for feedback, and maybe not wanting to hurt my feelings or get too deep into the weeds, he didn't have much to say. What he did say, however, left me shaking my head from side to side with an ironic smile.

"You know, Tom, I've read through this and the only thing that's missing for me is—I don't really have a sense from reading this what you believe. There are little snapshots here and there, but in the end I'm not sure I have a clear sense of where you stand spiritually. And I think people want to know." Instantly, my mind traveled back 40 years to the question I had asked Bill, and the circular nature of life.

The issue for Sean—like me trying grasp Bill's faith—wasn't that he was missing the intellectual chops to find my faith throughout this book. After all, he's a double major in religion and music, Phi Beta Kappa graduate of the University of Colorado. Instead, I think I often sidestep faith rather than walking straight forward. It's because I am at best, a reluctant evangelist.

While I strive to seek the things that Jesus sought, I want people to have open minds. I want Word and Spirit and life to fill their hearts and minds, not me or anyone else who thinks they have the answers. I want people to find their own answers on their own time, and my desire is simply to be a humble partner.

In short, if people are thirsty, I am happy to tell them about life changing waters that can quench their spiritual thirst. However, I have no interest in going around telling people they are thirsty. And there's a big difference between the two. Having offered that, I nonetheless believe I'd be something of a wimp if I did not respond to Sean's call to share what it is I believe. Here goes.

I believe there is a Spirit we call God.

I believe Spirit is present in the world today.

I believe the life and teachings of Jesus provide the foundation for how to live.

I believe as followers of Jesus Way our primary job is to bring his teachings and values to the world.

I believe there is a spiritual realm that exists beyond this life.

I believe that as humans we often fall short of being the people God calls us to be.

I believe that there are no limits to the love that God has for us.

I believe it is our job to respond to the gift of life by doing God's work.

I believe we are called to not just accept grace, but to extend grace to others.

I believe we are called to be stewards of all creation.

I believe we have everything we need to make this life *amazing*. It's just that people like me—and you—keep messing it up.

A final thought. If you are really interested in what I believe, it strikes me that you'd probably also be interested in what has been the greatest challenge to my faith. Simply put, I've spent *way too much time* trying to figure everything out. Questions like, "just how involved *is* God in the world today?" During my first 25 years of ministry, questions like this made me crazy, and most of time time I felt like the world's worst minister because I did not have the answers I felt I should.

Conversely, the best thing that has happened in my faith in the last 15 years? It's been accepting that much of life and much of faith is a mystery—that I do not need to have all the answers. And neither do you.

Poems & Tunes

Garage Sale Buddha

July, 2006

In 2006 our family made our first visit to Telluride, Colorado. Telluride's beauty is jaw-dropping, and the entire community so enticing that we gave serious consideration to making it our home after I was given a very tempting job offer in 2007. While we made the decision to stay in Lake Bluff and Lake Forest, Telluride remains a very special place, particularly Hotfoot—the Clarke family home outside of town where we have been blessed to stay.

Hotfoot 2006

Hotfoot is an evening gaze
at bold southern peaks
still telling the story
of a sun long set

Hotfoot re-minds
amidst mountain air, twinkling stars, kind rain
sun, moon, trees, birds, creatures, sounds
It's not all about me

Hotfoot questions
do the beavers know how glorious their estate?
the eagles how powerful their gift of lift?
does the hummingbird treading air, right there
visit just for joy?

Hotfoot is a trance
staring at slow motion,
early morning elk
for whom meadow is bed and breakfast

Hotfoot is curiosity
wondering when deceptive clouds
will decide to collide
and send daggers reaching across the sky

Garage Sale Buddha

Hotfoot is peace
rare like the air
where a spent soul
is massaged back to life

Hotfoot is a place
where with each step outside
you venture deeper and deeper

Hotfoot is grace experienced.

May, 2010
With thanks to Posy

Beachbound Waves

tiny ripples happily freelance
a flowing rhythmic water dance
headed for a new destination—
an aqua re-creation
they're beachbound waves

as they get near shore
from behind—a mighty roar
it's a rolling wave ten times their size
the other waves have unionized!

the little waves that took their time
had no choice but to join the line
no longer free & independent
they were pushed & went where they were sent

as the water tube rolled toward shore
the surging wave started to roar
at its crest it began to curl
the top of the wave white as pearl

but now at its destination
a power-filled wet creation
the bold wave got tripped by the land
and spread out thin all over the sand

Garage Sale Buddha

for the wave the beach was a dead-end street
life's no fun when you're flat as a sheet
the beach turned out not so sweet
time to make a hasty retreat!

so what roared like a lion left like a lamb
sliding back to the ocean after the slam
the wave knew it belonged to the sea
that was where it was meant to be

so if you find yourself beachbound, that's ok
explore for a moment, make time to play
but get back to deep water while you have the chance
'cuz the ocean's calling for the next dance

May, 2005
Written on the 35ᵗʰ anniversary of my father's death, it's a true story from start to finish, and I sing it—often tearfully—at each Father's Day Worship on the Beach Service.

New Old Spice

When I was a little guy, and just old enough to stand
I wanted to be just like my Daddy when I grew to be a man
He always had a smile and a sparkle in his eye, plain for all
to see - and a contagious kind of enthusiasm that inspired
my friends & me

So when Father's Day came it was a special day, a time to
be extra nice - to tell my Daddy I really loved him, & give
him some New Old Spice

And every year he'd say "What a surprise - how could you
have known? Last year's bottle is just about empty - where
could it all have gone?"

Well the years went by and I became a teen, and I went off
to high school - my friends would complain about their
"old man" but my Dad kept being cool

Oh, sometimes he would cheer too loud, when rootin'
from the stands - but even as a teen I wanted to be like my
Dad, when I grew to be a man

Then in May back in '71, the world crashed in on me - my
Dad suddenly went to a better place, despite my frantic
pleas

I cried out "Oh God what have you done?" I'd never felt so
bad - I couldn't imagine continuing to live, without my dear
young Dad

Well every June came Father's Day, and I never knew what
to do - so I'd say a simple prayer to him, "I still want to be
like you"

As the years went by it started to seem, I'd never get to
be a Dad - which I rationalized and accepted, but deep
down it made me sad

There'd be no New Old Spice for me, and I thought that
would be OK - I devoted my life to other things, until one
special day

The doctor handed me a package, a very special delivery
"You got yourself a little boy, congratulations you're a
Daddy!" (then I asked my wife)

"Can we name him after my father, if it is all the same?"
Jean answered "I know you love your Father, but Clarence
won't be our baby's name"

So we settled on Tommy Jr., cause not much goes with
Dickelman - I'm over 25 years older than my Dad ever got,
but I still want to be like him

Now, bring on that New Old Spice, I'll slap on all I can
Maybe Tommy'll be like my Dad, when he grows to be a
man...when he grows to be a man

October, 2003

One day Kerri Sherman shared this wonderful true story of her son Noah coming home from preschool and quietly going to the back yard, ostensibly to save the penguins of the world after hearing about global warming at school. I turned the story into a song, and Noah's dad Derek later wrote a children's book and the whole story was turned into a segment for WGN TV by Larry Potash.

Noah's Song

The earth is getting warmer, but not because of the sun
And I want to save the penguins, each and every one

This is the story of Noah, a tale that's never been told
He's a five-year-old little guy, with a heart of gold

He likes to play with friends, and his sister, too
Noah does real well with sharin', when he's at preschool

Well one fall day at school, as nature colored the trees
Noah was doing some coloring, when the teacher said
"Attention please"

"Please put down your crayons, it's time for a stor-ee
So come on gather all around, and sit on the rug with me"

Now Noah and his classmates, sat cross-legged as kids do
The teacher waited 'til they were quiet, and said
"Here's the story for you."

"The story I have to tell today, is both sad and true

Garage Sale Buddha

it's about where all the penguins live, who don't know what
to do

The teacher went on to tell the tale, of a penguin family
Living on a polar ice cap, far from you and me

How they swam & fished & waddled about
And always found time to play

But how the very ice on which they lived
Was slowly melting away

As the teacher looked at the children, with heavy heart she
shared
The story of a warming earth, and the penguins who need
our care

You see she knew it would be the kids, sitting cross-legged
on that rug
Who'd somehow have to fill in, the ozone hole we dug

refrain
The earth is getting warmer
But not because of the sun
And I want to save the penguins
Each and every one

Well Noah heard the story, it settled into his heart
He had an idea of what to do, and he couldn't wait to start

When he got home from preschool, he was a very different
boy
'Cause Noah was on a mission, there was no time for toys

He gathered all the things he would need, from kitchen and garage, too
Noah wanted to help those penguins, he had to see what he could do

Well he went outside and got to work, as his mom wondered
"Where's my boy?"
He wasn't in front of the television, or playing with his toys

Soon mom found her son Noah, in the middle of the back yard
She saw by the holes he'd dug in the grass, that he was working hard
But using her mother's instincts, she left her son to be
She knew something special was happening,
She wanted Noah's dad to see
A few minutes later Dad came home
Mom said "Go out and see your son
Noah's in the backyard—Go see what he has done"

Well Dad had no clue what was up, but walkin' outside he found
A backyard filled with piles of dirt, and little holes in the ground

And next to the hole Noah was working on
Was a bucket he had found
It was filled their freezer's ice cubes, Noah was planting in the ground

"Dad, I am planting ice cubes, so the earth will get real cold and then the penguins won't die, they'll be there when I'm old."

refrain

The earth is getting warmer
But not because of the sun
And I want to save the penguins
Each and every one

2010

I wrote this song—a favorite of mine—in response to the crazy world in which we live. It seems like we're always trying to do more and more, and often at the same time. I like to sing this in church, and listen to the congregation sing the refrain which sometimes has a soulful feel, as if to say, "You're right—we got the blues, brother!"

Multi-Tasking Blues

There's way too much going on, I have too much to do
if you don't watch out, I'm gonna multi-task you
I've got the multi-tasking, multi-tasking blues (we're multi-tasking, multi-tasking)
If you don't watch out I'm gonna multi-task you

I'm the cook and the cleanin' lady, and I tutor every day
I'm the full-time chauffeur who drives them to school and NVA
I work a f/t job, and all the bills I pay
There's way too much going on, and all that's left to say is

I've got the multi-tasking, multi-tasking blues (we're multi-tasking, multi-tasking)
If you don't watch out I'm gonna multi-task you

I went to see a therapist, it was the healthy thing to do
"You go too much on your plate" she said "that's why you're feeling blue!"
She said, "I feel your pain—I'm sorry you're in such a state
You either have to remove some food or get a bigger plate"

I've got the multi-tasking, multi-tasking blues (we're multi-tasking, multi-tasking)

Garage Sale Buddha

If you don't watch out I'm gonna multi-task you

I got pulled over in my car, I asked "Officer what did I
do?"
He said "You were speeding, and talking on the phone, too
The stereo was blaring, and steerin' with your knees
All while you were eatin', a quarter pounder with cheese

*I've got the multi-tasking, multi-tasking blues (we're multi-tasking,
multi-tasking)*
If you don't watch out I'm gonna multi-task you

Well, I even multi-task at night, when I'm lying in my bed
I listen to those Ted Talks, whisper in my head
While I've got an appliance in my mouth, and wrinkle
cream on my face
So I am ready at 5:00 a.m. to start my daily race

*I've got the multi-tasking, multi-tasking blues (we're multi-tasking,
multi-tasking)*
If you don't watch out I'm gonna multi-task you

So, I got so much to do, I want to leave nothing to chance
So I make to-do lists, the dry cleaner finds in my pants
But I have them all backed up, on Mac and my PC
Come and join my wireless network, and multi-task with
me!

*I've got the multi-tasking, multi-tasking blues (we're multi-tasking,
multi-tasking)*
If you don't watch out I'm gonna multi-task you

Now, you're doing it right now, as you listen to what I say

Your mind is starting to wander, about what you'll do today
But what I should be doing, while I'm down here on the beach
Is begin an all-new journey—and practice what I preach!

I've got the multi-tasking, multi-tasking blues (we're multi-tasking, multi-tasking)
If you don't watch out I'm gonna multi-task you

Garage Sale Buddha

August, 2002

I wrote the Community Song for our church when we began meeting on Sunday mornings in the autumn of 2002. It seemed clear to me that we'd never be a great singing church, primarily because we come from so many different spiritual backgrounds and places. In short, we don't know the same songs. Catholics, Jews, Lutherans, Presbyterians, you-name-it, all generally sing different songs. So, I figured we needed a song we could all get to know and sing well each week (that wasn't Amazing Grace or Kum Ba Yah). I wrote the Community Song for our church as a simple, spirited song we could all get to know over time and learn to sing well! Over the years, I have been absolutely blown away by how "real musicians" have taken my simple, four-chord blues shuffle and turned it into lively way to begin worship.

The Community Song

We're here to worship, our Creator today
We're here to worship, our Creator today
Lord open our hearts, let us hear what you have to say

We make a joyful noise, as we sing out our song
We make a joyful noise, as we sing out our song
Lord lift us up, and carry us all day long

Now still our hearts, as we offer up our prayer
Now still our hearts, as we offer up our prayer
Lord strengthen us, help us feel your love and care.

Garage Sale Buddha

December, 2015

*Like many folks, I'm really drawn to Leonard Cohen's "Hallelujah."
I don't begin to understand the lyrics, which strike me as bizarre and
just this side of Richard Harris' "MacArthur Park." But the tune and
refrain? Fantastic. I've written new lyrics for this moving song—in my
case, for the Christmas season—with a bit of a progressive, universalist
spin.*

"Christmas Hallelujah"

The world 2000 years ago, was like it is today, you know
With people just trying to find their way
Searching high and searching low, looking for which way to
go
They sought a king they hoped would bring Hallelujah
Hallelujah, Hallelujah, Hallelujah, Hallelujah

Then to the world came a big surprise, a bundle full of
baby's cries
His mother, not married, just a teen
Joseph was a humble man with the courage to take a stand
They raised the boy & we sing Hallelujah
Hallelujah, Hallelujah, Hallelujah, Hallelujah

Well 30 years after Bethlehem, the child he became a man
He sang a song that most people couldn't hear
Faith is more than following rules, a loving heart is your
best tool
Live in the light and you'll sing Hallelujah
Hallelujah, Hallelujah, Hallelujah, Hallelujah

He reached out to one and all, he labored to destroy the
walls
That keep us from being family
Brown or white, rich or poor—he's knocking on every
door
Saying—grace brings new life—Oh Hallelujah!
Hallelujah, Hallelujah, Hallelujah, Hallelujah

He sang his song for just three years, crucified amidst tears
& jeers
The Spirit lives to help us find our way
If you love God Christian Muslim & Jew,
Buddhist Hindus & agnostics, too
Then Jesus—he'll be singing Hallelujah
Hallelujah, Hallelujah, Hallelujah, Hallelujah

Today it's up to you and me, to live our lives in unity
We're brothers, we're sisters, one and all
If the world trends another way, Spirit gives the courage to
say
There's just one family—**SING IT!!!—HALLELUJAH!**
Hallelujah, Hallelujah, Hallelujah, Hallelujah
Hallelujah, Hallelujah, Hallelujah, Hallelujah.

Mother's Day, 2009

When it comes to keeping things clean and straight, I am inconsistent at best. At times I'm like the Felix in the "Odd Couple" and have all my shirts in the closet lined up in the same direction, arranged by color. I like that. But my default is probably far more as Oscar— someone who does not devote a lot of time to keeping things spiffy. This song was written around Mother's Day while I was doing a rare deep clean, but begins with the messy room I typically had as a child.

Mother's Day Song

Tommy come here, come here on the double
From the sound of Mom's voice I knew it was trouble
She bent down low to get into to my face
"Your room's a disaster, it is a disgrace
There are so many clothes all over the floor
It's pretty near impossible to open the door
To your room…"

"Until this is cleaned you are going nowhere
And if you don't like it I haven't a care
I don't like the word, but you are a slob
And don't try and blame it on your brother Bob"
And then she used the word as only Moms can
I knew it was comin' so I almost ran
"I'm *disappointed…"*

And that's my life's story since I was a teen
Trying to keep my room and life clean
Once in a while it goes real good
I pick up my socks and put away what I should
I feel real bad things are usually a mess

Garage Sale Buddha

Even though I know what is next to godliness
That is *cleanliness*

Well recently I took a new lease on life
Convinced it was good for my family and wife
I straightened with the passion of a crazed young teen
My friends started to say "Hey you're Mr. Clean"
I'd dust and I'd vacuum while I'd sing a song
And Jean got scared & asked "Is something wrong –
"Are you OK…"

I tackled the garage with a feverish pitch
I held onto a broom like a Halloween witch
As I cleaned the garage I sang, "This feels good"
I'm doing all those things I knew that I should
As the rummage pile grew I started to feel free
I was taken a leap toward simplicity
Then it happened…

The last place to tackle was my clothes closet
That I'd ever come out was an uneven bet
Well, I tried on some shorts amidst my old tees
The only problem was I couldn't get 'em past my knees
And I saw a favorite sweater and a bowling shirt or two
But when I got to my t-shirts I didn't know what to do
I was dazed….

And I unfolded those t-shirts and read every one
They told the life story of my Father's son
As I looked at those t-shirts I began to cry
The story of my life was there—right before my eyes
Places and races printed on my old t's

Looking at them was like readin' my
Autobiography

So, I had a heart to heart with the man in the mirror
The message I heard was abundantly clear
Don't give away everything in your quest to be free
You can keep your t-shirts from 1983
The holy black T from a Mac race long ago past
And the Chicago Triathlon where I came in   *Almost last*

So, I left my t-shirts right where they are
I made my mini more truck than a car
I went to the Army but not for salvation
I'm giving them my old stuff, I am a new creation
I sure hope it is as good for them as it is for me
They got some of my past and I got simplicity
But not my old T's...

So, if you are thinking about doing a Spring Clean
Don't let it become an unfortunate scene
For cleaning should not fill you with strife
it should lessen your load and give you new life
& it's ok to hang onto what you can't give away
old t-shirts are holy in more than one way
you know it's true..

Garage Sale Buddha

Spring, 1983

I wrote this and sang it for the seminary community my senior year at McCormick at the annual Feast of Fools Dinner. I came in second that night in voting for the #1 Fool, losing to the winner Professor John Burkhart, for whom I wrote this song after he spent the semester assigning ridiculous amounts of work to his students.

Bible Totin' Clone

Work my fingers to the bone
Becoming a Bible totin' clone
Doing what the experts say I should
Not having time to think, if it's good

And I ain't even making pocket change
And I got no furniture to rearrange
And I might have to go out and get a job that pays
Or I can go on welfare so I can get a raise

Somethings ringin' but there ain't a sound
Keeps my head spinnin' all around
Some folks here it after there's been a fall
Must be God with a long-distance call
Saying I want you for my ministry
Please don't turn your backside to me

And I ain't even making pocket change
And I got no furniture to rearrange
And I might have to go out and get a job that pays
Or I can go on welfare so I can get a raise

I say this is crazy what's happening to me
Why, even the good Lord, had one day free!

Garage Sale Buddha

The Profs don't argue but they do say "Son,
God never took time off 'til all the work was done!"

And I ain't even making pocket change
And I got no furniture to rearrange
And I might have to go out and get a job that pays
Or I can go on welfare so I can get a raise

Say What?

Community Church Group,
Victoria Falls, Zambia, 2020

Garage Sale Buddha

Life Quotes

"My last name is Delman. D-E-L-M-A-N. It's like Dickelman without the 'ick.'"
—Elliott Delman.

"Is this really a song we should be playing?"
—My words to bandmate Terry Moran and fellow members of the Dancing Bohemian Ukulele Team as we played our closing song—Bob Dylan's "Knocking on Heaven's Door" at the Lake Forest / Lake Bluff Senior Citizens Annual Beach Breakfast—attended primarily by folks in their 70's, 80's and 90's.

"Did you get the guy? You know, whoever put his cigarette out on your forehead."
—My Florida marina neighbor Don, with stitches in his head from a recent Key West bar fight, checking on my well-being after noticing ashes on my forehead following an Ash Wednesday Service I attended.

"Are you guys in the race?"
—An awkward question posed by the skipper of another sailboat during a race in Lake Geneva as they lapped rookie crew member Kraig Moreland and me racing in my J22 "Quad Dog".

"You're in the wrong room, jerk bait!"
—My brother Bob at Leonard's Funeral Home in Glen Ellyn after discovering me at age sixteen standing respectfully in front of an open casket—and wondering, "Why our grandfather didn't look at all like he used to."

"Dis rock."

—A half-drunk groom holding up a jumbo-sized diamond for his platinum blonde bride-to-be, in response to my question, "Sir, what token of your love do you give?"

"If you know how to swim, it takes longer to drown."

—My marina friend Don, explaining why he never learned to swim. Don was a certified Coast Guard captain who delivered boats around the world—but had never learned to swim. I had been teaching him to windsurf in a back bay in Ft. Myers Beach, Florida, and had to rescue Don, whom I thought was joking around, but in reality was starting to drown after he fell and the current took his boat out of reach.

"You can't use Pine Sol to clean the inside of a refrigerator!"

—My boss yelling at me after I used the incredibly fragrant cleaner inside a rental condo unit's refrigerator while living on my sailboat *ELLA* in Florida and working weekends cleaning condos. About $200 worth of groceries for the vacationing family had to be replaced.

"Hi. I'm Jimmy Olsen."

—My first college roommate introducing himself after showing up ten days late for college due to "parole issues." It turned out Jimmy was a 27-year-old ex-convict who'd just been released after spending 22 months in prison for holding up a Chicago liquor store with a hunting knife.

"We are sorry, you did not pass German. However, you pass."
—The German professor and the School Director telling me at the end-of-the-year party at Salzburg College that while I flunked the class, they appreciated that I tried hard and did not cheat like many other students. So, they passed me, with the one proviso being that I promise to never take German again.

"Half of you go to that basket, half of you go to that basket, and the rest of you come with me."
—Glenbard West Sophomore Basketball Coach Bob Jones directing his team at an early season practice.

"Actually, I'm living in a five-bedroom house on Sanibel that's on the Gulf of Mexico—with a part-time housekeeper who does my laundry and keeps the fridge stocked."
—My response to a friend on the phone who expressed concerned because the last anyone had heard after I resigned from my ministry in Indiana was that I was unemployed and living somewhere in my car. That had been true, until my dear friends Johnny B. and Barbara Smith offered me their Sanibel home for the winter while I rehabbed a sailboat I purchased in nearby Ft. Myers Beach.

Garage Sale Buddha

Church Quotes

"You know, I pretty much believe what everybody believes. That 'God so loved the word that he gave his only forgotten Son.'"
—A parishioner at a church I served who wanted to follow me to my next church and become our Assistant Minister. (I asked him, "What do you believe," and he replied by reciting a curious variation of John 3:16, exchanging "*begotten*" with "*forgotten*.")

"Join us for Ash Wednesday prayers and ashes this Thursday."
—From the Community Church Sunday bulletin in February 2019.

"If Jesus was a Jew, how come he had a Mexican first name?"
—Words I read scrawled on a bathroom stall my first day at San Francisco Theological Seminary.

"By his Apostles, God has instructed that a man shall leave his wife and cleave unto his mother…"
—At a wedding early in my ministry, when I inadvertently swapped the words "wife" and "mother" in the wedding liturgy. As it turns out, the marriage ended in divorce and the groom did end up living with his mother for a time.

"Tom—shorts, a Hawaiian shirt, and Birkenstocks are not how you dress for a wedding rehearsal."
—Senior Minister, boss, and spiritual father Bill Enright explaining to me that my dress at the very first wedding rehearsal I led following my ordination was not exactly

appropriate at the cathedral-like Second Presbyterian
Church of Indianapolis.

"God Dammit!!!"

—A phrase I almost never utter, screamed, while throwing
a full coffee mug across my new church office denting the
wall and splattering coffee everywhere. I'd just been told by
the Presbyterian Church Synod Executive she would not
accept the results of my alternative Bible Content exam—
despite providing everything they asked for—including a
hand-written outline of the *entire* Bible.

"Don't worry, I'll write you a recommendation to get you in any seminary in the country."

—The late Rev. Howard Rice, beloved Chaplain at San
Francisco Theological Seminary and former Moderator of
the Presbyterian Church in the United States of America,
writing to roommate David Wettstein and me after we
almost got kicked out of seminary for creating a not-so-
underground, tongue-in-cheek look at seminary life via a
newsletter we called "The Average White Boy."

"Sorry, but do you mind backing up a little bit?"

—Me, about to throw up from dizziness at my own
ordination service. I became dizzy and nauseous as people
swarmed around me for the laying on of hands ritual—all
due to an inner ear infection called labyrinthitis I
contracted two days before ordination.

"Thank you very much. Thank you very much."

—The only feedback I heard after the first sermon I
preached in seminary, titled "Soaring Above the Clouds of
Doubt." I later found out that virtually none of the thirty or

so people present that day in the Asian Methodist congregation in Oakland, California, spoke English.

"Love me tender, love me true..."

—The song of an Elvis imitator, complete with poofy black hair, white jumpsuit, and quivering upper lip at a funeral I led on Chicago's southside. The departed gentlemen was somehow squeezed into his WW II uniform and on full display in an open casket, while two childhood friends stood at attention nearby in their uniforms— complete with fake rifles. All I could think was "if my friends from seminary could see me now."

"The Community Church? Why yes, we are very diverse. We have a wide range of white people."

—The late Elliott Delman, musician extraordinaire, humorist, and Community Church communications manager joking about our 95% white ethnic composition.

"Not only did the Apostle Paul have a problem with women, but I think it's very likely that he was gay."

—A Harvard-trained psychiatrist and participant in a Bible study on Ephesians 5 ("wives submit yourselves to your husbands") that I led to kick off a new church year. The study included one very conservative woman who just moments before had said, "If it's in the Bible it's true, I believe it, and we ought to do it!" Fortunately, she was hard of hearing and did not catch the comment on Paul being gay.

"We'll have an open bar from 1:00 to 3:00 p.m.—and then you say a few prayers."
—My friend Barb telling me what she had in mind after asking me to lead her husband's memorial service.

"Lighten up, Francis."
—Words I muttered aloud, quoting Sgt. Hulka from "Stripes," after I received a letter taking me to task for a Center for Innovative Ministry session I titled "Innovation: Like a Pirate Ship Sailing Into a Yacht Club?" The letter's author wrote "I'd like to point out what I thought all grownups knew: that piracy is criminal violence at sea. Criminal violence as practiced by pirates typically includes murder, rape and torture—all in pursuit of the primary purpose of theft." OK, I get it. Lighten up, Francis.

"Did I really just hear that—at a wedding?"
—A question I asked myself after I officiated at the wedding ceremony for a very sweet Puerto Rican, Roman Catholic couple (who could not get married in their parish church because they had a child out of wedlock). After the vows, the bride's fifteen-year-old sister played a strangely familiar song that I recognized as the theme from "M.A.S.H." The song's title? "Suicide is Painless."

"Why, Tom, I think you mist yo' callin'—you shoulda been an actuh." (*offered by a sweet, 85-year-old lady with a deeply southern accent*)
—The greeting the late Elizabeth Peters gave me following a particularly lively sermon and worship service. I tried to take her words as a compliment.

"Tom, we think it would be best for you to keep the furniture off the roof."

—The late Bill Olsen, Building Manager at the cathedral-like Second Presbyterian Church of Indianapolis, after I had moved a small table, chair, my popcorn machine, and phone through my office window onto the third-floor roof to spend the afternoon making phone calls...and catching a few rays.

"It'll never work."

—Esteemed Professor Carl Dudley sharing his opinion on my vision for the Micro Church, which would eventually become the 350-family Community Church.

Garage Sale Buddha

Acknowledgements

I am grateful to many for the roles they have played in my life and ultimately in the creation of *Garage Sale Buddha.*

My wife Jean, for her love and supporting yet one more goofy idea— my need to write this book.

My Mom Lois Anderson aka "Pengy" for all the ways she has quietly helped me live a Kierkegaard life.

My sister Sue Sullivan, whose presence I truly miss and whose life continues to inspire me, and her always gracious husband Brian.

Tommy Dickelman, Jr., Kate Stuckslager, and Annie Stuckslager who are among the greatest blessings in my life.

Bill Enright and Charlie Alcorn, who inspired me to become a minister when I was still a teenager, who've steadfastly modeled the life of faith to me for over 50 years, and who along with their amazing partners Edie and Sandy have always treated me as family.

Kraig Moreland, not only as good of a buddy as I've ever had but also my publisher and indispensable guide in producing this book.

Jay Sharman, a treasured friend who is a sounding board, steady source of encouragement—*and whose book is next!*

Sean Miller, Co-Pastor of the Community Church, golfing buddy, and confidant who is a blessing each day we work together.

Editor Margaret Kelley, who not only helped make *Garage Sale Buddha* readable but whose insights were instrumental in the creation of this book.

My brother Bob, a skilled writer who helped me think through the cover and other parts of this book.

Bill Bartolotta, for creative and soulful encouragement over "Beer & Fries" at the Lake Bluff Brewing Company.

Phillip Ross, whose gentle disposition and design expertise were a perfect combination at just the right time.

Lifelong friend Stu Meacham, who has been an invaluable advisor to our family for 40 years.

My devoted and lively co-workers and partners at the Community Church as I wrote this book: Daryl Beese, Pam Campbell, Patrick Chan, Kate Cole, John Corrigan, Elliott Delman, Tommy Dickelman, Ken Hall, Zach Hancock, Teddi Koch, Sean Miller, Steve Rashid, Mary Jo Stevenson, and Peter Wolff.

Fellow Lake Forest / Lake Bluff Pastors Mike Woodruff of Christ Church, Luke Back of Church of the Holy Spirit, and Clint Roberts of First Presbyterian for their spirit of cooperation and collegiality.

Jerry Osher, Doug Campbell & Jim Fondriest—each of whom has been an extraordinary caregiver and friend.

John Borta for arriving "just in the nick of time" to guide us with myriad technical issues in publishing *Garage Sale Buddha.*

To Southminster Presbyterian Church and First Presbyterian Church in Glen Ellyn, Illinois for introducing me to the life of faith, and to San Francisco and McCormick Theological Seminaries for blessing me with life-changing educational experiences.

Finally, to Monkey Boys past & present for their incredible support of our ministry and me personally. Charlie Clarke, Cindy Corrigan, Chris Fisher, Tim Hender, Ross Jannotta, Ned Jessen, Peg Moreland, Matt Nagel, Kent Street, and Geoff Woie—our church and my life would not be what they are without you.

Made in the USA
Monee, IL
13 March 2023

29470344R00134